Strategies for the Threshold #4

Hidden in the Cleft:
True and False Refuge

Anne Hamilton

Hidden in the Cleft: True and False Refuge
Strategies for the Threshold #4

© Anne Hamilton 2019

Published by Armour Books
P. O. Box 492, Corinda QLD 4075

Cover Image: © Can Stock Photo / iloveotto; © istockphoto /
Rasica
Section Divider Image: © istockphoto / timonko
Interior Design and Typeset by Book Whispers

ISBN: 978-1-925380-14-9

A catalogue record for this
book is available from the
National Library of Australia

Strategies for the Threshold #4

Hidden in the Cleft:
True and False Refuge

Anne Hamilton

Other Books By Anne Hamilton

In this series

Dealing with Python: Spirit of Constriction
Dealing with Ziz: Spirit of Forgetting
Name Covenant: Invitation to Friendship

Devotional Theology series

God's Poetry: The Identity & Destiny Encoded in Your Name
God's Panoply: The Armour of God & the Kiss of Heaven
God's Pageantry: The Threshold Guardians & the Covenant Defender
God's Pottery: The Sea of Names & the Pierced Inheritance
God's Priority: World-Mending & Generational Testing
More Precious than Pearls:
The Mother's Blessing & God's Favour Towards Women
(with *Natalie Tensen*)

Mathematics and Theology in Medieval Poetry

Gawain and the Four Daughters of God:
the testimony of mathematics in Cotton Nero A.x

Award-winning Children's Books

Many–Coloured Realm
Daystar: The Days are Numbered Book 1
Merlin's Wood: The Battle of the Trees 1

Thank you

Dell
Donna
Gloria
Ian
Joy
Mark
Michael
Monika
Quang
Rosemary

Contents

Introduction   ix

1   **Coffee & Other Forms of Self-sabotage**   1

2   **The Hound of Heaven**   20

3   **Strange Havens**   45

4   **First the Raven, Then the Dove**   60

5   **The Limitations of Repentance**   80

Summary   102

Endnotes   104

Introduction

For almost two centuries, Christians have spoken of 'false refuges'—self-created havens away from God. In recent years, practitioners of mindfulness, particularly in the Buddhist tradition, have picked up the term. So too have psychologists. Each has given it their own spin.

Originally, however, the concept comes from the prophet Isaiah and goes back over 2700 years. People have been looking for sanctuary and shelter away from God since then—and even longer! Isaiah, however, contrasts the false refuge with the Cornerstone that God will lay in Zion. In fact, he makes it clear that there is a connection between such refuges and covenants with the enemy of our souls.

This is the fourth book in the series, *Strategies for the Threshold*. The first two volumes discuss the tactics of the spirit of Python and the spirit of Ziz to blockade the path into our calling. Perhaps their most successful strategy is to tempt us into a false refuge.

Many people are convinced they do not have a self-created haven away from God. And, even if that is a remote possibility, they are certain their covenant is with God, *not* with any unholy spirit. However, *if* you haven't come into your calling and have experienced relentless spiritual opposition as you've tried to do so, it's not a question of *if* you have a false refuge and a counterfeit covenant. It's a question of what kind it is.

This book shows how seemingly innocent and innocuous false refuges can be. As usual, as for all my books, this work is designed in numerical literary style, using a mathematical pattern to construct sub-sections. It emulates the word-number fusion that sits in the background of the gospels and epistles. Hopefully, you won't even notice this device.

People often ask me, 'How do I start? What is the first step I should take to come into my calling?'

My answer always is, 'Identify your false refuge.'

And that is what this book aims to help you do.

Anne Hamilton
Brisbane, Australia 2019

1

Coffee and Other Forms of Self-sabotage

'Sometimes I sits and thinks and sometimes I just sits.'

Lucy Maud Montgomery, *Anne of the Island*

When I was much younger, I loved the *Anne of Green Gables* series. And whenever I was upset and my mum asked me what I was doing, I'd use this quote from one of the books. 'Sometimes I sits and thinks,' I'd say, 'and sometimes I just sits.'

I grew up and, as happens for most of us, life threw me some major disappointments. Serious heartache came my way. And to deal with it, I did what I'd always done. Sometimes I would 'sits and thinks'. But sometimes, when the pain was too great, I would detach myself from the thinking and just sits.

After a while, I found it was easier to sit with a cup of coffee and sip it slowly. People looked at me less dubiously and asked fewer questions that way. I discovered it's much more socially acceptable to stare vacantly into space with a cuppa in hand.

Time went by and, one after another, failures and

frustrations piled up. After each disappointment or disillusionment, I'd sits and thinks for a while—sometimes a short while and sometimes a long while—then eventually I'd pick myself up and move on. Sometimes it wasn't about moving on, sometimes it was about trying again.

I'd always felt that I had a call on my life to be a writer but one rejection followed another and another and another... for twenty-seven years. The setbacks and challenges were relentless. At the beginning of my journey, I naïvely thought that, as long as my writing was good enough, it was simply a matter of persistence before I could find a publisher.

Eventually I realised that being a mathematics teacher wasn't helping me. I didn't have the right network of influential friends to help me come to the notice of a publisher. So I'd go along to writers' groups but, as soon as I answered the natural question about my day job, I was the instant outsider. The conversation would stop cold, as if number-wielding and algebra was a close cousin to axe-wielding and mass murder. People just don't know how to relate to you if you've got an affinity for mathematics and they haven't.

So I doubled down, worked harder, invested in developing my talent. I took the plunge and signed up for an exceedingly expensive external studies course in creative writing. However the start of the course was delayed, first for a few weeks, then for a month, then progressively for eighteen months because of the lecturer's unavailability. When it was finally off and running, I found that I was barred from participating. On investigating, I discovered that, according to the fine-print in the rules of this prestigious Christian college, I should have withdrawn from the course before the end of the first semester. Technically therefore I'd 'failed'. In fact, as it transpired, my record had a gross failure recorded on it. Given that the circumstances were so unusual, I was told I could apply to get the bar lifted. But to re-enrol would require me to pay both a penalty and the full course fees again.

It was one of those times I did the sits-and-thinks-and-drinks-coffee thing a lot.

I decided to cut my losses. Instead I eventually found a small class, highly recommended, run by a Christian author with a couple of spectacular writing awards to her name. I paid the fees and got one lesson before the class mysteriously folded and the author could not be contacted.

I did the sits-and-thinks-and-drinks-coffee thing a whole heap more.

A few years down the track I decided to have another go at external study. I started on a creative writing course at a different Christian institution. Half way through one semester, just as I sent in the third of four major assignments, I received a phone call from one of the lecturers to tell me that I'd mistakenly been sent the wrong study notes. The subject had been entirely revamped—and was now so different that the options were limited as to how this could be addressed. I was given the direct line for the head of department and told to contact him immediately. Mindful of my previous experience with technically 'failing' by not withdrawing, I rang back straight away. And every two or three days after that, I phoned again. I left messages on his answer phone and I rang his office repeatedly, asking his assistant to drop a note on his desk. Late one evening about six weeks later, I got a phone call from the head of department. He was tidying his desk as he chatted with me and kept coming across one after another of those notes. He thought it was funny. Perhaps strangely, I couldn't see the lighter side of it. Because, after a delay of six weeks, my options were now *seriously* limited.

More coffee. More sits. More thinks.

I had actually self-published a book by this stage, so I decided to accept the recommendation of the head of department to simply be granted recognition of prior learning.

That book was *The Singing Silence*. Twenty books later, I'm only now at the stage where I've recouped the losses incurred in printing it. Before I took the plunge and printed *The Singing Silence*, I put in a full year of research which involved contacting store owners and stockists, retail buyers and wholesale distributors of all stripes. I asked their preferences and I asked why they would turn down a potential book. I took all their advice and I avoided everything they'd flagged as a negative. I tailored it carefully to meet all the preferences and requirements they mentioned. Despite all this effort, most bookstores turned me down flat when I tried to find stockists.

So I did considerably more of the whole sits-and-thinks-and-drinks-coffee thing. It became increasingly clear that being accepted for publication by a traditional publishing company was the only way forward.

Now I'd like to be able to say that, at the end of the day, God rewarded my patience, my perseverance, my long-suffering and my refusal to accept rejection. That's what I'd like to be able to say, but it wouldn't be true.

The fact is that, in all those decades of trying to find the key to the locked door into the world of publishing, I had become weary of all the effort. I was heart-sick and disappointed. And a lot of that disappointment was with God.

In the twenty-fifth year of this struggle, I happened to be visiting my parents when they lived in Caloundra. We went to church together one Sunday morning. During the service, another visitor stood up and asked if he could give a word of encouragement. 'There is someone here today,' he said, 'who has remained faithful to the call of God on their lives but, after years of working towards that calling and diligently seeking the open door, they are so blocked, they are no nearer than when they'd first started.'

Now, normally, when someone out the front asks for others to come forward for prophetic prayer, I hesitate. *Surely*, I think, *there are lots of people here in a worse position than I am.* So I look around and, by the time I realise I probably am the one the person out front is talking about, I've lost the opportunity. Someone else has jumped in ahead of me.

So I looked around this Sunday and—to my disbelief—

no one else was responding. I was stunned. Finally, a message from God directly for me. *For me.* And everyone around me seemed to know it—my parents, as well as other people, were pushing me forward. 'It's you!' they whispered. 'He's talking about you!'

So I went out for prayer that morning and, as a result, I thought my breakthrough was imminent. But it still didn't come... and didn't come... and didn't come. And didn't come.

And didn't come.

A year went by.

Hope had revived, only to be more seriously dashed than ever. I had been crying to God, 'How long? How long?' but now I gave up. I came very close to believing I'd spent my whole life in grandiose delusion.

The wisest man who ever lived, King Solomon, described my state of mind perfectly in Proverbs 13:12 NIV, *'Hope deferred makes the heart sick.'*

It doesn't matter what breakthrough you're longing for: restoration of a marriage; reconciliation with a brother, a mother, a lover; physical healing of a long-term illness or disability; the end of a financial mess; the opportunity to launch out of a job that grinds you down; or a shift in circumstances that are so soul-destroying they make you sick with despair. Eventually we all reach that place where we know we can't hold it together anymore. That last thread of hope snaps and we realise that it's excessively unlikely anything will ever change. We've been plodding along, steadily facing forward and waiting for the light at the end of the tunnel to appear. But there's no sign of it. We come to the conclusion the tunnel is blocked. So we let go of the dream.

And, somewhere along the line to that final moment of resignation, it's natural to become disappointed in God.

'How long, God? How long?'

That's the silent, desperate cry of our heart. The thing about being disappointed in God is that, in Christian circles, it's as socially unacceptable as staring vacantly into space without a cuppa in hand. So, it's best to tell no one. To keep absolutely quiet about it. It's better still to convince yourself that you don't feel that way at all.

Me? Disappointed in God? No way. How could you possibly think that?

The stage is set for the entrance of denial. I gave denial such a starring role in my life that I even denied my denial. I just wasn't aware it was so deep a problem that it was one of the major hindrances to every breakthrough. I had a ready-made list of excuses to hide behind every time another rejection letter arrived in the mail:

'I guess I didn't hear God's voice, after all.'

> This was hard to reconcile with the promise of Jesus that His sheep hear His voice in John 10:27 but not too hard. I had developed quite a fine line in rationalisations. I figured that I'd ignored His voice when I'd heard it and had instead listened to the

desires and ambitions of my own heart. The trouble was that, no matter how hard I prayed, the desire to write didn't go away. At one stage, I decided that the only way forward was to give up writing entirely. My thinking was that, if I made the sacrifice for a year, then at the end of the time, some other activity more in line with God's will would come to fill the time I'd freed up. But twelve months later, to my immense surprise, nothing had. Even I could recognise the unnatural void in my life.

'Maybe I didn't have enough faith.'

Even though God tried to thump my head against the wall trying to beat this out of me, I still succumbed to this pathetic excuse. At one memorable time, I'd decided to enter a competition. I wasn't expecting to win but I had total faith I would make the short list. And I mean total, perfect, impeccable, untainted faith. It was such an extraordinary experience of God buoying up my feelings that, even when I tried to doubt, I couldn't. Did I make the short list? No, of course not. I was devastated. Because I realised that, if my best work couldn't make the short list, then I had no hope of ever seeing my dream come true. *Besides something's incredibly wrong*, I thought, *if I have 100% faith when we only need a mustard seed's worth*.

'Maybe I didn't pray the perfect prayer with exactly the right words.'

As if it's ever possible to pray perfectly! And as if

Jesus isn't the perfect mediator who translates my weak and imperfect wording to the Father. And as if the Holy Spirit doesn't take the inarticulate yearnings God put in my heart and, as Romans 8:26 says, prays them for me with groans too deep for words.

'Maybe it's my motivation that's the problem.'

Yeah, yeah. As if I'm going to have completely unsullied motivation this side of heaven. I can't fix my motivation—I can only surrender it to Jesus, to bless and break and use it as He wills.

'I shouldn't have listened to the negative voices.'

This was a late addition to my list and my flirtation with it was fairly brief. However, at the time it made its temporary appearance, I was coming across increasing numbers of Christians who were saying it was important to surround yourself with people who spoke encouraging, edifying words that promoted faith. That prophecy should always be affirmative and uplifting. It didn't take too long to ditch this idea. Scripture from Genesis to Revelation is full of rebukes and calls for repentance and confession that are designed to prick consciences, not lull them. Besides, I realised, it's not positive thoughts that determine the breakthrough, it's Jesus. And if anyone says that the positive thoughts are merely to reinforce faith, they've misunderstood. Yep, I'd actually learned a thing or two as a result of having to delete my excuse about not having enough faith. And what I'd learned was this: I could have faith that stretches from one side of the galaxy to the other and it still wouldn't be enough to impress God. Ultimately it's not about *my* faith, it's about the faith of Jesus as I cling to Him. It's the faith of Jesus, as He represents us before the Father, that God responds to in His grace. I only need a crumb. We're *not* saved by faith. We're saved *by grace* through faith.

'It can't have been God's will.'

Assuming, of course, that God's will is always done on earth as it is in heaven. Why would we be asked to pray for it in Matthew 6:10, if it were a foregone conclusion? It is not God's will, for example as Peter reminds us in 2 Peter 3:9, that anyone should perish but that all should have eternal life by coming to repentance.

And then there was my all-time favourite, go-to excuse whenever things went from bad to worse:

'It seems God is teaching me patience.'

You see, I knew that nice trite little cliché about, how if God is making you wait, you're in good company—David had waited about 15 years for the throne, Joseph had spent 13 years as a slave or in prison, and Moses had been sidelined for 40 years in the desert. Still and all, my day job was teaching mathematics so I was able to do a bit of calculation and projection. I figured that, at the rate I was going, I would have to live longer than David and Joseph, but not quite as long as Moses. My writing career, if I'd estimated correctly, was going to take off somewhere between the ages of 110 and 120 years old.

My faith was fast disintegrating to crumbly rubble. No, perhaps that's not quite true. My faith in faith was shattered. In addition, my faith in my own picture of God was tottering. I didn't recognise how much He was standing in harm's way for me, or how much He was at work in my life, stripping away rationalisations, shredding misconceptions, confronting me with my excuses.

All I knew was that He hadn't answered my prayers, hadn't responded to my faith and had not fulfilled what seemed to me to be specific, personal promises.

I didn't realise I was upset with Him. In fact, I was completely oblivious to the fact I was so disillusioned.

Perhaps there was an aspect of God's grace in not knowing. Because, as a result, I began talking to Him one Sunday evening when I was sitting with a cup of coffee. Not thinking. Just staring at the fluttering curl of rising steam. Yep, just doing the habitual sits-and-thinks-and-drinks-coffee thing once more.

I'd just come back from a meeting with a group of writing friends. There, I'd told them about my most recent rejection. And in return they'd told me—as they often did—what an enduring inspiration I was. How encouraging it was to see someone who, after 27 years of disappointment, still hadn't given up. They praised me for my persistence, tenacity, resilience. They spoke consoling words and patted me on the back for my determination and my stubborn, never-say-die attitude.

I didn't tell them how close I was to giving up. That I had started to believe that I was totally deluded about my sense of a divine calling to be a writer. I allowed their soothing words to wash over me as I sat with that cup of coffee. I wasn't thinking, just brooding mindlessly.

That gave way after a few minutes to a talk with God. I started out by simply thanking Him for the gifts He'd put into my personality: persistence, tenacity, resilience, determination, stubbornness, a never-say-die attitude. All the things I'd heard my friends praise me for.

And, perhaps because I was at last, after all that time, in a responsive state and intentionally engaging with God, rather than detaching myself from all feeling, I heard an unexpected sound. To this day, I will swear that—at that moment—I heard heaven laugh.

I was so surprised, I listened more closely.

'You?' God snorted at me. 'Persistent?' The laughter got louder and I sensed it coming from more than one Person. 'Really? Tenacious? Resilient? Stubborn?'

I was startled. For some reason, heaven found what I'd said uproariously funny. *But... but...* I thought. *These aren't my words. They are the words of my friends. It's not as if I'm self-assessing.* 'Err...' I began with a bit of trepidation. 'What do You think?'

And He said, 'Well, whenever you are disappointed, you know what you do? You make yourself a cup of coffee, then you sit with it. You sip it slowly. You brood over it. And, if the disappointment is particularly severe, you might distract yourself with a good book or some comfort food. Then, once the disappointment fades—which might take anything from a few days to a few months—you pick yourself up and try again.'

Nailed it, I thought. *Couldn't have put it better myself.*

'And what,' I asked God with just the tiniest bit of indignation, 'is wrong with that?' *Like: what is the problem? I'm not doing drugs, sleeping around, getting smashed on alcohol or viewing porn. I'm just sitting with a cup of coffee.*

'You've never come to Me and asked Me what went wrong.'

I almost choked on my coffee. 'But... but... I thought I didn't have enough faith. I thought I was out of Your will or Your timing or the words of my prayer weren't specific or positive enough. Or that I'd heard Your voice wrongly. I thought You were teaching me patience.'

'Teaching you patience? You acquired that decades ago! The problem now is that you don't know when to stop being patient. It's an excuse for doing nothing.'

My heart sank. Everything God was saying was completely and absolutely and undeniably true. My head was stuck in the theological space of wondering how anything could possibly be wrong that God couldn't fix. However, it also couldn't refute what He'd said. It was a fact I had never gone to Him and asked Him what went wrong.

From the bottom of my heart, I apologised to Him. At least, it felt like the bottom at the time. I was to find out later that there were still considerable deeps to plumb.

I repented. I told Him that I wasn't going to do it again. I was going to make the turnaround and come to Him first, not to coffee. He was truly going to be my refuge in times of trouble, nothing and no one else. I asked Jesus to empower my words—because, unless He did, I'd be sitting and thinking and sipping lattés for the rest of my life instead of stepping into my calling.

And, at that moment, I had a sense of relief. *It's all over*, I thought. *Finally. Now the big block is removed, the breakthrough is going to arrive any day.*

But it didn't. And it still didn't. In fact, I got another rejection letter in the mail. My heart sank. I sighed.

Still, having learned my lesson, I went to God. 'Here I am,' I said. 'I've come straight to You. Aren't You proud of me?'

I learned in that moment that God might have dealt with my false refuge of coffee but there was a lot of work that needed to be done with regard to spiritual pride.

'What went wrong?' I asked God.

I discovered right then and there what a wonderful, loving Father He is. He said, 'Let's discuss the problem over coffee.'

It wasn't actually coffee that was the problem—or even sitting, with or without thinking. It was that I'd substituted them for a relationship with God. And once I started to talk to Him, He was quick to answer. I'd got so used to waiting decades for answers to prayer that, when they started to come in a matter of days, I was unprepared for the swiftness of the response.

Anyway, this particular day, I discussed the problem with God over coffee. He didn't console me. In fact, He directed my attention to the wording of the rejection letter I'd been sent—He pointed out some subtle nuances and ambiguous phrasing. He said quite forthrightly, 'It is the intention of those who've assessed your work to steal your idea. To cherry-pick the concepts they think are right and dismiss what is, in their view, wrong. They've even made clear their intention, if you've the astuteness to read between the lines.'

I was horrified. As soon as God pointed out particular sentences, I could see what He was talking about. And I knew He was right—because I'd had my ideas stolen more than once in the past. 'This always happens to me,' I said, 'whenever I put even a toenail over the line into an area for which I'm not qualified.'

This always happens to me... I was abruptly taken aback by my own statement. It contained the word, '*always*'.

Now I'd received enough prayer ministry to know what an '*always*' statement meant. It almost certainly indicated a vow. I considered the statement, turning it around and around in my mind. I reworded and rephrased, reshaped and reframed it until it sat just right and I was able to identify the vow: *I will always be robbed whenever I step into an area where I'm not qualified.*

Now although this felt so very right, there was an incredibly deep wrongness to it too. Vows, generally speaking, are born out of traumatic childhood experiences. Yet no child ever says to herself: 'I will always be robbed whenever I step into an area where I'm not qualified.' Children don't think that way; they simply aren't qualified for anything! And they wouldn't have a clue when they'd crossed a boundary from 'qualified' to 'unqualified'.

Besides, qualifications—at least from a human perspective—shouldn't have any impact whatsoever on any spiritual calling! I knew the old saying: *God doesn't call the qualified, He qualifies the called.* And I believed it utterly. Because, as far as I was concerned, there was an extremely good reason for God operating this way: if we were qualified to do the job He has for us, we'd rely on our own strength, not His. Any calling He has for us is so far beyond us that it's imperative to rely on Him. If our first instinctive response to Him when He presents our calling to us isn't 'No! I can't do that! That's way beyond me!' then it's probably not our calling.

Still, if being unqualified was—ironically—the first qualification for a divine calling, then a vow about being robbed due to lack of qualifications was going to be an Everest of a problem as I tried to step into any calling.

I had to get rid of the vow. But where had it come from?

If it wasn't a childhood vow of mine, then it had to come down from one of my parents or grandparents. I went to my mum and asked her if anything like this had happened to her. She shook her head. 'What about dad?' I asked.

My dad had died several months previously so there was no opportunity to ask him directly. 'He never mentioned anything,' my mum said.

'What about his mother or father? Or your mother and father?' I asked.

Mum knew of nothing. It was a total impasse. God had answered me but, within less than an hour, I was back to the stumbling block once more.

But then the next day, everything changed. Just everything. I was completely unprepared for the swiftness of God's answer. Even today, nearly ten years later, my mind is habituated to the idea that it's necessary to wait patiently on God for decades. So when He does answer straight away—as He increasingly has—I'm startled by the immediacy of His response. In fact, there have been times I've been caught out by it. 'Next time You plan to answer right off,' I've said to Him, 'could You let me know in advance? Just so I can be ready.'

But back to my world-tilting day—a day that happened just twenty-four hours after I went to God for the first time instead of to coffee. It came about like this: my niece had recently got her driving licence but she wasn't confident negotiating traffic. She wanted to go to a prayer ministry course but she was a little anxious about driving all the way across to the other side of town to attend. So I volunteered to drive her. Although I'd done that particular course twice before, I decided that rather than drive there and back again and then repeat the trip to pick her up in the afternoon—which would take at least four hours out of the day—it would be more convenient to stay there. So I enrolled once more.

When the time came for small groups, the leader decided that I was going to me the one to receive ministry. I tried to protest. I suggested that there were others who'd never done the course before who should be before me. However the leader wouldn't hear of it. So I racked my head for a problem that needed solving. I explained to the group about my desire to be a writer, my belief that God had called me to it and my weird vow about qualifications that seemed to have no basis in my own life or that of my ancestors.

The leader frowned in sudden pensive thought and, opening her Bible, she began flipping through the pages. I thought she was going to read me an encouraging Scripture but instead she pulled out a strip of paper. She read it out: *whenever I was about to receive a reward for my hard work, someone with more qualifications would cut in and push me out, taking the promotion I'd earned.*

'Yes!' I exclaimed. 'That describes the situation almost exactly. Where did that come from?'

'Those are your father's words,' the leader said.

I stared at her in disbelief. *What were my father's words doing in her Bible?*

'I went to visit him just a couple of months before he died,' she said. 'And when he said that, I thought, "You'll want to deal with the issues behind that when you recover," so I wrote them down to make sure I could speak to him later about what he'd said. They've been sitting in my Bible ever since.'

To say I was stunned is to vastly underrate my feelings. Yes, of course this was God's perfect timing, of course, of course and of course again. However my mind was reeling at the myriad of tiny decisions needed to not only place me in that group that day but to cause me to open up about that exact problem. And so to discover a generational vow that came down my father's line.

As I was renouncing this vow, I heard the Holy Spirit speak. 'While you're at it,' He said, 'you might also renounce your covenant with Death.'

Huh? What on earth is that? 'The Holy Spirit is talking about the covenant with Death,' I said to the leader, hoping she could explain. But she had no idea. She shrugged and held up her hands.

'Ok then,' I went on, 'I have no idea what a covenant with Death actually is, but I'm just going to follow this prompt.' So, out loud, in front of witnesses, I renounced a covenant with Death.

And everything changed.

Human history is the long, terrible story of man trying to find something other than God which will make him happy.

CS Lewis, *Mere Christianity*

2

The Hound of Heaven

Where do you go when life slings a disappointment at you and your first instinct is to fling yourself into the arms of serious comfort? What do you do to soothe your wounded spirit? How do you behave? What consolations do you seek and indulge in?

I probably wouldn't have understood the enormity of the problem in my behaviour had not the Holy Spirit sent me the prompt: 'covenant with death'. When I looked that phrase up in Scripture, I found it mentioned twice in Isaiah in connection with a 'false refuge'.

Now it so happened that I knew what a 'false refuge' was. I had encountered a teaching by Gloria Roberts, formerly of Elijah House Canada, where she spoke of how difficult it is for people who are mainlining hard drugs to break the chains of their addiction. She had revealed that the spirit of heroin says, 'I am your friend,' and it's necessary to break the power of that agreement before healing can begin.

Such an example unfortunately engendered a snug feeling of security—it had always previously seemed that a 'false refuge' was linked to hardcore addiction. However, it's actually linked to simple habit.

God had made it clear to me that He was not my refuge in times of trouble. A cup of coffee was.

A false refuge is basically a place of solace away from God in times of disillusionment, disappointment, rejection or crisis. They can be as innocuous and as seemingly innocent as a chocolate bar. They can range across an entire spectrum from totally destructive to deceptively harmless.

> *Almost every man has a refuge, that is, he has something in which he has put his trust to comfort him. The difficulty with most men is not so much that they have not a refuge, as that they have a false refuge, a refuge that will fail them in the hour of crisis and need.*
>
> RA Torrey

When we're troubled, we're tempted to find the kind of false refuge Torrey describes. And unfortunately, if you're like me, you've congratulated yourself on overcoming this temptation because you've avoided the obvious pitfalls: you haven't soothed your hurt feelings with a truckload of alcohol or sought relief by viewing internet porn.

When we classify some behaviours as spiritually 'safe' and others as 'dangerous', we miss the sin that often stares us in the face. Instead we instinctively think of ourselves as conquerors just because we're not consoling ourselves with drugs—either illegal or prescription. And we may even quietly believe we've got the situation beat if we don't lick our wounds by gambling away the entirety of the family budget in a single sitting.

So what if we eat a whole tub of ice-cream? Binge watch movies? Shop 'til we drop? Fake it 'til we make it? Distract ourselves with a good book? Zone out for a couple of days?

Who are we hurting by any of these things?

The last one is a very common behaviour for modern men. They just simply check out mentally. They'll even tell their wives: 'I'm just going to zone out for three or four days. You can try to talk to me but no one is home. I'll be back by the end of the week.'

Isn't it far better to do this and dissipate the frustration rather than to put a lid on it, letting it build up to an explosion?

Or what about the guys who are so crazy go-go-go busy that the only time they get to slow down is when they slip off to the bathroom? And there they sit, getting a few minutes of downtime by scrolling through the social media feed on their phones? Isn't that better than burnout?

Know what? This is **not** going to God. This is not seeking Him first as your strong tower, it's not hiding in the shadow of His wings, it's not running to Him as your refuge and strength day in and day out.

To make matters worse, false refuges like these are associated with a covenant with Death:

'We have entered into a **covenant with Death**, *with the realm of the dead we have made an agreement. When an overwhelming scourge sweeps by, it cannot touch us, for we have made* **a lie our refuge** *and* **falsehood our hiding-place**.'

Isaiah 28:15 NIV

The Living Bible clarifies this same verse:

'You have struck a bargain with death, you say, and sold yourselves to the devil in exchange for his protection against the invaders.[1] *"They can never touch us," you say, "for we are under the care of one who will deceive and fool them."'*

The Nature of Covenant

Now, at this point, you're probably thinking to yourself: 'Hold on! I haven't made a covenant with Death. I've never gone to the devil and asked for his protection.'

This is to totally miss the point about covenants. You don't need to have made one personally. If one of your ancestors raised such a covenant—and if no one in the intervening generations has revoked it—it's still legally binding over your life. A covenant is far, far more than a contract: for a start, it has no end-date, no termination clause, no conditions for annulment. Covenants go on forever. The covenants God raised with Abraham have passed down through his descendants, generation upon generation, to the present-day.

Sure, you can violate the covenant and bring down a

whole raft of curses on your head. But violation is not the same as revocation. You might be breaking the terms of the covenant, but you're not severing it off.

A second difference between covenant and contract, and perhaps the most crucial one, is that a covenant involves oneness. So a 'covenant with Death' is not simply an agreement that can be split off at any time, it's a state of oneness that requires the intervention of God to dissolve.

A covenant with Death means this: at some point in a family's history, someone has experienced so much sorrow, despair and loss that they've turned their back on God. They've said to themselves, 'God is not all-loving and He's definitely not all-powerful. The most powerful being in the entire universe is Death. I know what I'll do: I will covenant with Death for my own survival and that of my children. Death will be our protector.'

This is of course deeply perverted thinking. Expecting Death to protect us against itself is unimaginably warped as well as totally illogical. But in the stress of grief, people do things that are irrational—things that in their saner moments they regret. Yet later, when time fades the scars on their soul, they may not even remember entering into such a covenant. Only the evidence will remain: from generation to generation, all the family ever receives in life is survival. Because generation after generation, we remain complicit with the covenant, even if we are not consciously aware of its existence.

Now, think about these facets when it comes to the oneness

aspect of this covenant: can Jesus—*The Resurrection and the Life*—be truly one with us while we are one with Death? Can He—who is also *The Way, the Truth and the Life*—be totally one with us while we are one with Death?

Life and Death in unity? No way!

If God hadn't told me that my behaviour was associated with a covenant with Death, I would never have realised it. It would always have seemed too extreme to think I'd sold myself to the devil for a cup of coffee.

I mean, I know everyone has their price—*but...!* Come on. Was mine so dismally and pathetically low? Apparently it was.

And as I read Dallas Willard's comments in *The Divine Conspiracy*, I realise this just shows what a typical part of the human race I am:

> *Now in fact, the patterns of wrongdoing that govern human life outside the Kingdom are usually quite weak, even ridiculous. They are simply our habits, our largely automatic responses of thought, feeling and action. Typically, we have acted wrongly before reflecting. And it is this that gives bad habits their power...*

> *They do not, by and large, bother to run through our conscious mind or deliberative will, and often run exactly contrary to them. It is rare that we want to do wrong as the result of careful deliberation.*

> *Instead our routine behaviour manages to keep the deliberative will and the conscious mind off balance and on the defensive.*

Weak, even ridiculous—that describes most false refuges perfectly. Going back to Isaiah 28:15, let's note that it not only mentions that a lie is our refuge but also points out that falsehood is our hiding-place. The Hebrew idea behind the word for '*hiding place*' is the concept of having an idol.

My false refuge was coffee. Once God revealed it was linked to a covenant with Death, He was effectively declaring: it is your idol. And an incredibly worthless one at that.

Jonah 2:8 NET reminds us: '*Those who worship worthless idols forfeit the mercy that could be theirs.*' And Psalm 16:4 adds that our sorrows will be multiplied when we choose idols instead of God.

Whenever I read these verses now, I feel like thumping my head on the table. How could I have been so dim-witted as to forfeit God's mercy for, of all things, a cup of coffee? How could have jeopardised God's covenantal defence of me for such a trivial reason? How could I have so foolishly allowed my pain to be multiplied so mindlessly?

Especially since, as it turned out, I didn't actually have to give up coffee—I just had to relegate it to its proper place in my life. Now of course the same will not be true of all false refuges and their associated idols: for example, God is probably going to give the okay to diffusing essential oils while we're chatting with Him but certainly He isn't going to say to any of us that we can use tarot cards or continue seeing a clairvoyant as an adjunct.

Complicity

I have no idea which of my ancestors took out this covenant with Death. In fact, I don't need to know. The issue was my complicity with the covenant. I'd never done anything about it. That was my passive complicity. My active complicity was through the vow that meshed in so well—I was in agreement with my generational bloodline about qualifications and calling.

God was battering at the walls of my life, trying to get me to see what the problem was. But was I listening? No, I was ignoring Him and throwing a tidy sum of money at a few coffee manufacturers. Still, when He finally had my attention, look at how swiftly He moved. As soon as I'd passed the test—and there will always be a test—as soon as I'd run to Him as my true refuge in disappointment, He had everything set up to give me the answer to my problem within twenty-four hours. 'While you're at it,' He'd said, 'you might also renounce your covenant with Death.'

Now you might think the breakthrough happened right away after that.

But it didn't. No. It was still some months away. Quite a few months, in fact. It was a season long enough to pull the heartstrings of hope right to their limit once again.

Then two things happened: first, the book I'd waited 27 years to see in print was accepted for publication;

and secondly, I was offered a job as a writer and editor, completely outside my sphere of qualification.

These both occurred on the very same day. The fact that they happened simultaneously really highlighted the occasion as a miraculous opening of the door into my calling. It was so self-evidently the final breakthrough that I was suspicious about the timing. So I did a countback to see how long it was since I'd renounced that covenant. I'm a numbers person and I have looked into many of the numbers in Scripture, so I realised there was a very deep significance to that particular count of days. In fact, as I've worked with other people to help them pass over the threshold into their own calling, this special number has recurred time and time again. I'm sure you're curious as to what it is.

However, I've only shared it on very rare occasions. There are several reasons for keeping it quiet: first, I don't want to put God into a box and suggest He has to follow a formula; second, I don't want you to fall into the expectation that there's a certain stretch of time you have to make it through and then, after that, all will be well; third, on the one and only occasion I have actually prayed for God to shorten this season for someone who convinced me she was absolutely desperate, the time period was lengthened by a week. I wondered, even as I was praying, if I was right to ask God for the shorter time or whether I was operating in unregenerate fleshly pity, and I felt I got my answer.

My conclusion is this: there is a genuine spiritual season

between renouncing a covenant with Death and seeing the breakthrough. Generally speaking, in my experience, this season is a uniquely fixed number of days—however I wouldn't want to claim that God is required to keep to this schedule. He is God, after all.

Why is this time period so long?

Well, words are cheap. Renouncing means nothing unless it is accompanied by restructure. God is looking for evidence of our recommitment to a relationship with Him along with the realignment of our lives. And relationship simply doesn't happen overnight.

So if you're blocked off from your calling and you're looking for an instant solution, I have bad news. There is none.

Because each of these steps takes time.

Identify the Refuge

First, talk to God. Ask Him to help you identify your false refuge. Don't get overly anxious about it all and take on a spirit of religious scrupulosity—let the Holy Spirit guide you into what He wants you to deal with at the present point in time. I certainly didn't get rid of all my false refuges before God allowed me to enter into my calling—I only got rid of those He identified for me. Later He presented me with other false refuges I needed to clear away. God isn't waiting for you to be perfect before He allows you to pass over into your destiny, He's waiting for you to show yourself committed to the relationship.

Confess

Acknowledge that you have a place of comfort away from God. Be specific about it. Be personal. Don't say in a vague and generalised way, 'Lord, I confess that I have a false refuge,' but instead name the sin for what it is: 'Father God, when I get worried by what's happening at work, I don't go to You for relief and reassurance. I take it out on my kids when I get home. My false refuge is abusing my family.'

Now it's far better to confess to another person, rather than just privately to God.

1 John 1:9 NIV says: '*If we confess our sins, he is faithful and just and will forgive us our sins and purify us from all unrighteousness.*'

James 5:16 ESV says: '*Confess your sins to one another and pray for one another, that you may be healed.*'

The distinction is a subtle one: in the first case if we confess to God, we are forgiven; but if we confess to one another, we are healed. I encourage you therefore to find some believers you can trust and to have the courage to be open with them about your false refuges and hiding places, so that you may be healed as well as forgiven.

Some Christians believe it is unnecessary to confess anything to God—and therefore we don't need to repent either. They hold that, because we have been made righteous through the blood of Jesus at salvation, we don't need to do anything after that point. It's all done at the Cross.

This, frankly, is creating a false refuge out of a theological position. Confession simply means *to come into agreement*. That is why we can confess that we've sinned and also confess Jesus as Lord. When we confess, we simply agree with God that, on the one hand, we've committed a sin and, on the other, that Jesus is Lord.

Yet there are people who consider these exhortations to confession by James and John as completely irrelevant. They have elevated their own understanding of the writings of the apostle Paul to such a degree that James and John are superseded. Indeed, there are some who elevate the words of Paul above those of Jesus, rationalising their views on the basis that Paul is post-resurrection and Jesus isn't.

It might have been the pre-resurrection Jesus who effectively taught us to confess our sins through these words, '*Forgive us our sins, as we have forgiven those who sin against us*' (Matthew 6:12 NLT) but it was the post-resurrection Jesus who said to the angel of the church of Ephesus: '*Return to Me and change the way you think and act, and do what you did at first. I will come to you and take your lamp stand from its place if you don't change.*' (Revelation 2:5 GWT)

Are we going to dispute with Jesus and say that we don't need to *confess*—that is, just *agree with* Him? And that we don't need to repent of losing our first love?

I don't apologise for saying that the hierarchy propounded by some authors and teachers which seats Paul at the top, followed by Jesus, is supremely dangerous. John is sometimes given a place on a lower tier but, most often, this ordering relegates the teachings of James, Jude and Peter to outer darkness. But let me assure you, ignorance of Jude and Peter's admonitions about spiritual warfare won't save you from catastrophe. In fact, most of the horrific consequences I've heard about that involve believers who've taken on the forces of the satan are the result of disregarding these warnings.

When we take a theological construct and pit it against a clear and unequivocal Scripture we have essentially created a false refuge. Scriptural verses should inform and reinforce each other, deepening our understanding of what God requires of us. Where there is an apparent contradiction, it's time to press into the original languages for insight.

In fact, on the matter of contradictions and looking into the original language, it appears Jesus tells us to pray about our false refuges in the Lord's Prayer. I wasn't aware of this until a friend from New Zealand asked me about the line in that prayer that says: *'Lead us not into temptation.'*

Joy wrote:

> One version says, *'Lead us not to the time of trial but deliver us from evil.'* As it is written it doesn't go with how a Heavenly Father would operate. I know God allowed Satan to strip poor Job but he came out the other side knowing, honouring and loving God so much

more. Is this anything to do with why he allows the threshold 'guardians' to remain?

I could see exactly what Joy meant by 'it doesn't go with how a heavenly Father would operate.' In fact, James 1:13 specifically states that God does not tempt anyone, so why would Jesus direct us to pray such an irrelevant thing?

When I looked into the Greek passage in question, it turned out that the word for 'temptation' has a dual meaning. The other is 'test'. That's why we have the alternative translation 'time of trial'.

The word rendered 'lead' from the Greek doesn't have any other major connotations. It can also be 'bring' or 'carry' but neither of those alters its fundamental sense.

However, a massive surprise is awaiting with the seemingly innocuous preposition, 'into'. It is immensely significant. This particular Greek word for 'into' can also mean 'in union with'. It implies oneness and therefore carries connotations of covenant!

Factoring all this together, the meaning of this part of the prayer that Jesus gave us is more like: 'and when You test us, prevent us from covenanting with the tempter.'

In other words, the model prayer Jesus gave us asks God to help us avoid false refuges, as well as the covenants and the idols associated with them. That makes so much more sense than *lead us not into temptation.*

After this long rambling digression on theology as a false

refuge, let's turn our attention back to confession. If we actually are so resistant to confession of sin that we can't bear to follow the Scriptural injunctions, then we'd have to conclude that either pride or shame has a hold on us.

Because if we can't agree with God, then we have an agreement with the enemy.

In terms of covenant, such an agreement would be described as a vow. And it is these ungodly vows that hold us captive.

Personal Vows

My vow in terms of my calling was a quite unusual one: *I will always be robbed whenever I step into an area where I'm not qualified.*

Most vows are a lot simpler than that. Some are framed positively, some negatively. Let's look at some examples of the latter. Note that, if they don't have an 'always' or a 'never', it's implied in the wording:

> 'I'll never be good enough.'

> 'No one will ever tell me what to do.'

> 'I'll always be blamed.'

> 'Sooner or later, a man is always going to cheat.'

> 'You can never trust a woman.'

> 'People are always going to rip you off.'

'Love never lasts.'

'God answers other people's prayers but He never listens to me.'

'I'll never be any good at maths.'

I'm going to use this last vow, not only because it's so common but because it's straightforward. Besides, as a former mathematics teacher, I have *vast* experience with it. Long before I was consciously aware of the concept of a vow, I instinctively knew enough not to challenge the power of such beliefs head-on.

Back when I was teaching high school, a new cohort of fresh-faced twelve-year-olds would line up each year and tell me with blind acceptance that they were no good at mathematics. They were so convinced of the truth of this statement it would have been pointless telling them otherwise. They wouldn't have been persuaded. After all, they'd told themselves the same thing nearly every school day for seven years, so the neural pathway of this well-established belief wasn't a vague and faintly marked trail, it was a deeply scored rut.

Now, most teachers when it comes to teaching algebra try to encourage their students by telling them it's easy. Yeah, right. Who'd believe that? I didn't fall into that trap. I told them my classes—and I usually had at least three of them in any one year—that it was hard. 'You've heard of algebra?' I'd ask. 'This is the tough stuff. The really truly tough stuff. I want you to pay careful attention to everything I say. Anyone not concentrating on this lesson will be getting personal tuition at lunch time. Got it?'

Now that last threat guaranteed I'd get five minutes with everyone totally focussed on the blackboard. Wanting more than that was an ask too far, given their attention span— but in fact five minutes was all I actually wanted. With just three hundred seconds of undivided attention I believe— yep, here's a vow from me as a mathematics teacher, just to prove not all vows are bad—that you can teach any person of average intelligence how to solve an equation. Most teachers create problems for their students because they try to make algebra intuitive. Now this is a good starting point but, unless the students are helped to figure out what mathematical process they automatically used to arrive at their intuitive answer, they'll get stuck in the usual slough of despond. Because when the questions get harder, intuition will no longer guide them. It's best to get beyond intuition by the end of the first minute by simply using big numbers— really big numbers. And it's better-than-best to spring a snap test at the end of five minutes to see how they're getting along. Ten questions—each worth 1 mark for working and 1 for the answer and pass mark being 18 out of 20. Use of calculators permitted. 'I'm testing your algebra skills,' I'd say, 'not your arithmetic skills.'

It would be extremely rare for any student not to pass. I'd feign incredulity. 'This is just wrong,' I'd say. 'You *all* passed? But this is *algebra*!'

It would have been fatally easy to fall into the temptation to say, 'See? You *can* do maths!' But a single positive experience won't overturn seven years of contrary belief.

However, if it's wisely used, it can be a drive a wedge into the smallest of cracks.

So instead I said, 'You must all have twisted brains! You can't do the easy stuff but you can do the hard stuff. Now that's impressively twisted.'

Now the average twelve-year-old back in the day would have worn a badge saying, 'I have an impressively twisted brain,' with huge delight. It would have been seen as a massive compliment. I didn't try the impossible—I didn't try to take down a vow that had been reinforced for years. I set about installing a new one right next to the old—one with the potential to push over all that had gone before.

Now this is a workable strategy when it comes to vows about mathematics because it's not exactly common to find a demon using such a vow to gain a legal foothold in a person's life. But it would be entirely different for a vow like: 'I'll never be accepted, no matter how hard I try.' At some stage, an opportunistic demon could happen on by at a traumatic moment and attach itself to this vow.

Just as many students believe they'll never be any good at maths but never actually articulate the vow, so many of us have beliefs that sit in the background of our thoughts and are never spoken aloud. 'I'll never be accepted, no matter how hard I try' is the kind of statement that doesn't need verbal expression, but can still be part of the warp and woof of life. When these vows are about relationships, they influence the course of every interaction we have with other people—and with God. When they are about destiny, they impact every aspect of our ability to come into our calling. They are the legal impediments used by the satan to block us from any breakthrough. While they exist, they form our personal input into any covenant with Death coming down from our ancestors—and by ancestors, I mean both father's line and mother's line as well as bloodline and adoptive. Until these vows are renounced our false refuge still remains. It stands tall and proud, housing a wide variety of idols.

Notice the way vows and false refuges interact together: coffee is not ordinarily anyone's idol—but it was mine because my vow enabled it to be so.

It is our vows that power the search for a means of comfort. Once the means of comfort becomes habitual, we have created a false refuge and provided the opportunity for an idol to take up residence.

Today, many Christians like to declare and decree blessings for themselves and others. This is a very powerful practice—but it's a waste of breath when we're declaring and decreeing in contradiction to vows that have been repeatedly reinforced in our lives. Then it's about as effective as applying a band-aid to cancer.

Declaring and decreeing when it's used as a method of avoiding repentance is a false refuge. It's very similar to the theological hierarchy which justifies ignoring what James and John say in their epistles, simply because Paul doesn't talk about confession. He might not have used the word more than once—and *repent* not at all—but his constant exposure of sin in churches is a call to return to God.

Generational Vows

As the name suggests, generational vows are accepted statements that flow down unchallenged from one generation to the next. They're like a family motto: a belief system that cannot be extinguished and that often transcends both logic and experience. Generational vows engender unexamined beliefs that foster racism, sexism, elitism, political bias, religious bigotry, ethnic hatred and the like.

I had a friend at university during the seventies. A third-generation Australian of Irish descent, she was immediately able to identify the root of the problem whenever there was any mention of 'The Troubles' in Northern Ireland: 'It's all Oliver Cromwell's fault.'

It took me a while to figure it out. When it came to politics in Ireland, Cromwell—despite having been dead for three hundred years—was always to blame.

It's generally easy to identify generational vows. They aren't the sort of things a child thinks. Just like my vow, 'I will always be robbed whenever I step into an area where I'm not qualified,' they use the language and concepts of adults.

Nevertheless, it's worth checking out whether a generational vow is lurking behind a personal one. 'I will never amount to anything' might be the rewording of a teacher's curse or even a mother's. But it might equally be a reformulation of a belief passing down from an ancestor who was utterly convinced 'no one in our family will ever amount to anything.'

Generational vows hinder us stepping into our calling and they have to be chopped down for us to make headway. A perfect example of this is Gideon. God chose him to rescue the people of Israel from Midianite raiders—yet his first task was not to gather an army around him. It was to hack down the idols his father had set up.

This is exactly the family dynamic that imperils most of us. We haven't taken an axe to the idols revered by our family. We might have dealt them some blows and knocked off a few limbs but we've never allowed Jesus in to reduce them to splinters. Until we do that, and until we allow Him to build an altar to God in their place, we're going to be continually blocked off from our calling.

Governing Vows

A governing vow is a vow that overarches all others. It is often extremely difficult to detect. It's the pre-eminent and principal vow that determines the fate of other vows. Tackling a minor vow without addressing a governing vow is like uprooting weeds in front of an advancing steam roller.

Now it's quite likely that, even if you are familiar with the concept of a vow, you may never have before heard of a 'governing vow'. It is my own personal terminology.

Until I was ministering to a person who was affected by Satanic Ritual Abuse, I had no idea that such a vow existed. But during the ministry, the man made this comment: 'I will never do anything to trigger the programming.' By this he meant that he would never do anything that would activate the satanic indoctrination he'd received to go on a violent rampage and, amongst other things, commit murder.

It occurred to me that, because the programming was demonic, then such triggers could include forgiveness, repentance and renunciation of covenants. So I asked him if all of the many words of forgiveness he'd spoken over the decades of receiving counselling were actually conditional on them not triggering the programming. He agreed that was the case. The same was true for repentance, for revocation of vows and for renunciation of covenant. In all the years he'd been seeing counsellors and prayer ministers he'd never spoken unconditionally about anything.

Now in fact, 'I will never do anything to trigger the programming' was in his case an exceedingly good vow. It was such a gold warrant safety insurance policy I wasn't willing to tamper with it. But, by its very nature, it also meant the programming could not be deactivated through forgiveness and repentance. My years of teaching algebra and looking for ways to undermine the vow that 'I'll never be any good at mathematics' now stood me in good stead. I knew there had to be another way. So we consulted the Holy Spirit who immediately gave us a wonderful strategy to deal with this governing vow: and that was to find and remove the triggers.

After this episode, I began to look for other governing vows. I wondered if they were unique to people troubled by SRA or whether they were more widespread. Ultimately I believe it's possible for anyone to elevate a vow until it reaches this level but, in general, most people don't seem to have an 'alpha' ruling the pack. Their various vows compete for priority depending on the circumstances of life.

Nevertheless I do believe one of the more common governing vows is simply this: 'I am never wrong' or its generational parallel, 'My family is never wrong.'

This vow is prevalent even amongst believers. It may not be obviously present because it has an inherent twist. People with this vow can usually forgive others but they cannot repent. That's why it can be difficult to unmask— because when we see forgiveness in operation, we tend to assume that the person will also be able to repent. But notice the distinction: forgiveness says, '*You* have done wrong,' but repentance says, '*I* have done wrong.'

If the governing vow is 'I am never wrong' or 'I am always right', then it follows that the idol of 'I' will not permit repentance, even while it is offering forgiveness. Those with this kind of vow may well agree we are all sinners— but only in a theoretical, theological sense, not in any way relating to them specifically or personally.

John Holliday, the founder of *The Indianapolis News*, is said to have become upset one day on spotting a spelling error in his paper: 'height' had been printed as 'hight'. When the original copy was checked, it was discovered that Holliday himself was the culprit. 'Well, if that's the way I spelled it, it must be right!' he exploded. So for the next thirty years, 'hight' was the way the newspaper spelled 'height'!

There's wrong and then there's inability to admit to being wrong. One of the more insidious aspects of this particular vow is that it often leads to presumptive judgment. In a situation where the person with this vow becomes aware that their behaviour towards others could be considered wrong, they justify their actions on the basis of what they discern those others will do in the future. Such 'discernment', if accurate, is a wanton abuse of the prophetic gift. Prophecy is given to us in such instances so we can warn and correct, not so that we can sit in judgment over another's possible future behaviour. In fact, such misuse of this divine gift defiles and corrupts it, effectively reducing it to divination. The defilement can, at times, effectively become a self-fulfilling prophecy: if, for example, a manager believes a worker under his supervision will eventually betray him and treats the person accordingly, it doesn't take much insight to see that the worker's innocent actions may be misinterpreted. What the manager most fears may come upon him through simple defilement.

Ultimately a governing vow only allows the removal of sub-vows that do not conflict with it. The generational version of this vow, 'My family is never wrong,' has a variation, 'Family is all,' which is particularly prevalent in some parts of Asia. Even pastors and elders will defraud, defame and even frame church members, leaving them with the prospect of a criminal conviction, in order to protect not only their immediate family but distant relatives as well.

Francis Thompson was recovering from opium addiction during the late nineteenth century when he wrote *The Hound of Heaven*, which perfectly describes our false refuges and the God who pursues us relentlessly:

> *I fled Him, down the nights and down the days;*
> *I fled Him, down the arches of the years;*
> *I fled Him, down the labyrinthine ways*
> *Of my own mind; and in the midst of tears*
>
> *I hid from Him, and under running laughter.*
> *Up vistaed hopes I sped;*
>
> *And shot, precipitated,*
>
> *Adown Titanic glooms of chasmed fears,*
> *From those strong Feet that followed, followed after.*
>
> *But with unhurrying chase,*
>
> *And unperturbèd pace,*
> *Deliberate speed, majestic instancy,*
>
> *They beat—and a Voice beat*
>
> *More instant than the Feet—*
> *'All things betray thee, who betrayest Me'.*

3

Strange Havens

The deepest need of men is not food and clothing and shelter, important as they are. It is God.

Thomas R Kelly

Having identified our false refuges, having confessed our reliance on them, having revoked our vows and asked Jesus to empower our words of renunciation, we're now ready to repent. Actually it doesn't particularly matter about the order—it's fine to repent and reverse the lies we've believed before renouncing vows. I personally just like this sequence.

Repentance

The simple definition of *repentance* is 'changing your mind'.

It's doing a u-turn, it's spinning around in an about-face, it's heading back towards God instead of away from Him. Yet again, theology has surprised me with its ability to masquerade as a safe harbour while again offering a false refuge with regard to repentance. Some people today say that because the definition of the Greek word used for repent, 'metanoéō', is *to change the mind* or *to change the inner man,* then outward actions are not required.

Jesus, however, declared that you'd know His disciples by their fruit. (Matthew 7:20) This means love, joy, peace, patience, kindness, goodness, faithfulness, gentleness and self-control. (Galatians 5:22–23)

So, if your 'change of mind' doesn't exhibit this kind of evidence, then it's questionable whether genuine repentance is at work. An authentic reversal of thinking of necessity has its outworking in a reversal of behaviour. No one until the modern era expected that a 'change of mind' would not show up as a significant transformation in a person's life. This is the mindset of systematic rationalism, not that of the ancient prophets whose cries of 'Repent!' meant a complete reset of behaviour and lifestyle.

Let's face it, this farcical manipulation of theological concepts is simply a smokescreen to avoid real repentance. It fools only a very few people—and, sadly, that's because they want to be fooled. More unfortunately, however, legitimate theology is sometimes used in an inappropriate way to side-step repentance.

Such a practice is 'declaring and decreeing'. Now, there's nothing inherently wrong with declaring and decreeing. Jesus did it. But He certainly didn't do it to avoid repentance. Let's look at an example: suppose you've grown up in a household where your older brother was the favourite and your dad never had much time for you.

You plot and you plan to get his attention but it backfires time after time, and eventually he tells you, 'You scum! You've been a schemer since the day you were born!' You're hurt by the curse he's spoken, you're mortally wounded by his scorn, you swear you're never going to treat your kids the way your father has treated you. Never. Ever. Ever.

But, yes, you've just reinforced your judgments about life with a vow. And a vow has power. It will rebound on you in two different ways: others will scheme against you as you've done against your brother and, in addition, you will wind up doing exactly the same as your father. In fact, despite the vow to never ever ever treat your kids this way, you'll have a favourite son. And just as you schemed against your brother and father, your other sons will conspire against your favourite.

Recognise the outline? It's the story of Jacob and Esau, but it's also the story of Joseph and his brothers. Just as Jacob used a goat to deceive his father, so his sons used a goat to deceive him about Joseph's death.

Would it have been possible for Jacob to *declare* he would not reap in the same way as he sowed? Could he have *decreed* this generational pattern would not flow down to affect his sons? Actually, no. The Scripture is clear: '*Do not be deceived: God is not mocked, for whatever one sows, that will he also reap.*' (Galatians 6:7 ESV)

Any attempt to declare and decree in such a way as to nullify this verse—and I know of people who have tried to do this—is not only mocking God but is, in effect, practising magic. Magic is simply the use of the divine creative principles found in God's Word and in the world against Him.

Declaring and decreeing is a divine creative principle, prophetic in nature, designed to bless or to warn. It is not intended to counteract God's revealed will in His Word.

In a similar way, many believers today ignorantly attempt to use the covering of the blood of Jesus to neutralise Scripture. Again this is effectively magic: the use of God's design for redemption in a purposeful attempt to cancel out His Word. The blood of Jesus is powerful and efficacious when applied through repentance but it is not meant to be used *instead* of repentance.

Because covenant is about oneness with another, because it's far more than simple agreement, then it's not a straightforward matter to revoke it. There are curses attached for so doing. This is why it's a matter to present to God for His help. After all, as we noted previously, you cannot genuinely be one with the Resurrection and the Life if you are already one with Death. In going to God and seeking His help to annul the covenant, it's wise to begin by renouncing the 'clauses' that you personally have made use of. Those 'clauses' are in effect the vows and judgments, the unbelief and unforgiveness that motivate you to build a false refuge.

The blood of Jesus can ultimately be used to cancel the covenant with Death, its clauses and sub-clauses.

However, it cannot be used to simply ignore that covenant. The blood needs to be applied through repentance.

And yet the human soul is incredibly resistant to repentance. So often, it's only when we're in the deepest, darkest pit—and we've exhausted every other option—that we turn to God and ask for His help.

And then we find out a terrible truth: we can't repent. It's impossible. We can reach a point where we want to. We can even set our will, firm and resolute, to accomplish that change of life that shows a change of mind. That's when we discover we just can't do it. We can't transform ourselves. The truth of Paul's assertion in Romans 7:15 NLT finally dawns on us: '*I don't really understand myself, for I want to do what is right, but I don't do it. Instead, I do what I hate.*'

With this realisation, the moment arrives when we recognise that, short of total surrender to God and trusting Him to accomplish the change on our behalf, it's not going to happen.

And total surrender means *total and unconditional*. That doesn't mean it has to be formal or ceremonial. It just has to be real and authentic. Jackie Hill Perry writes of the moment she turned to God in desperation:

> '*What You are calling me to do, I can't do it on my own, but I know enough about You to know that You will help me,' I said to God my new friend. I didn't know that the confession of my inability to please Him and the shifting of my*

> *back toward the sins I'd previously embraced*
> *was repentance. Nor did I recognize that*
> *my resolve to believe that He could be to me*
> *what no one else could, was faith. But it was.*
> *Without asking me my permission, a good God*
> *had come to my rescue.*

The reason we resist surrender is that we want God to fix the situation. But we don't want Him to fix us. We want God to clean up our mess. Instead He wants to clean us up. If He sorts out our problems, but doesn't sort us out, we'll be back in next to no time, asking for another fix.

In fact, this is how many believers talk today: they'll openly say they need a 'fix' of Jesus. As if His consoling presence can be dispensed at our convenience. As if He is not Immanuel, God with us. As if He is not *one with us*. Maybe—just maybe—that's exactly what this expression is revealing. That those who want a 'fix' of Jesus are acquainted with Him but actually don't want to yield to Him in a covenant relationship.

Jackie Hill Perry in *Gay Girl, Good God* makes the point that, although many Christians with same-sex attraction are desperate to be healed, it often doesn't happen. In her view, it's because they are willing to present their sexuality to God but that's the limit. They are not willing to surrender their entire selves to Him —and allow Him into all the complex issues of life that entwine with their sexuality.[2]

Repentance is saying sorry to God, asking Him for His forgiveness, declaring your intention to spin around and do a u-turn, as well as admitting your absolute helplessness when it comes to making that happen. It's handing your life over to Him and asking Him for His empowering grace to put your declared intentions into action. It's calling on the name of Jesus and the power of His blood to enable you to keep on keeping on when you want to give up.

In terms of false refuge, it's surrendering your entire life into God's hands—but particularly that attitude and accompanying habit that forms this counterfeit haven. God may reinstate it, asking you to put it in its right place in your life. Or He may ask you to never go there again. He may even ask you to destroy it.

If you've comforted yourself with chocolate, God may not ask for it to be sacrificed. If you've used yoga as a coping mechanism, He will almost certainly ask you to give it up—since it involves being 'yoked'[3] to a high level demonic entity. If you've sought solace in erotic literature or magazines, God may well ask you to destroy them.

It's His choice—not yours. That's what surrender means.

The Test

Some time after you've repented, there will be a test. There will *always* be a test. Often when you're least expecting it. Have you really given up your false refuge? Or is there still a lingering desire to keep it? When you are disappointed once more and tempted to hole up with your favourite comforter, do you go to God instead and say, 'Here I am!'

Only after you've passed are you ready to renounce your

covenant with Death—or any other covenant God has pointed out to you.

What happens if you fail? God is not going to give up on you because you didn't pass the test. He'll give you another chance... and another... and another. It's not God who gives up on us; instead we are the ones who give up on ourselves. We expect to pass the test first time and every time. Sometimes, however, God has to coach us for a while before we can go to Him first and bypass our false refuges. He may have to point out more than one issue that needs addressing before we can pass the test.

Now covenant, because of its oneness aspects, requires more than a simple 'no'. When you want God to cut off an unholy covenant from you, it's necessary to say that this is a forever 'no', an everlasting 'no'—in fact, it's a 'no' as permanent and unconditional as the covenant itself has been. To *renounce* a covenant has this connotation. So we go to God and we say words to this effect: 'Father, I renounce my covenant with Death and with the idols of my false refuge. I say 'no' forever to this union agreed to by my ancestors and I turn my back on my own complicity with it. I ask for Your grace to empower the words I have just spoken through the power of the cross of Jesus. My words mean nothing of themselves—but the blood of Jesus can cut off every last defilement of this covenant. And I ask this in His name. Amen.'

The test might be easy to pass. When it came to coffee, it was nothing more than a simple act of will for me to say, 'Not coffee anymore—I'm going to God.'

Later on, I faced much more difficult tests than this. But before that happened, God had a word with me. At the time He did, I'd already crossed over into my destiny, so what He said was completely unexpected: 'You need to repent of taking long baths.'

'Huh?' I said. 'I haven't taken a bath for over twenty years.'

The Lord repeated: 'You need to repent of taking long baths.'

I thought back to those long, luxurious soaks in scented bath salts where I'd sit back and read a novel, adding a bit of hot water as the temperature fell. 'Lord,' I said. 'Would You mind explaining? I don't want to start getting super-religious or hyper-scrupulous. Why would I need to repent of having long baths?'

'You've always been sensitive to the spirit world,' He said. 'Whenever you detected a lot of low-level demonic activity around you, you dealt with it by having a long bath. You know: bath is a symbol of baptism, of the flood of Noah, of the spirits in prison in the third chapter of the first epistle of Peter. You sensed that water affects a certain kind of spirit before ever reading Peter.'

'I think I get it. Long baths were a false refuge.'

'Correct.'

'But Lord... like I said. I haven't done this for twenty years. Why do I need to repent of it?'

'Because you *would* still take long baths, if you could.'

I searched my heart and realised God was right. 'Yeah.' I sighed deeply. And I did as He said. I repented.

Again, this wasn't a hard thing to do. Because I hadn't done it in so long, it wasn't tough to re-align my heart towards God. But I began to wonder why God had been so insistent that I repent of something I was unlikely ever to do again. As I sat and chatted with Him about it, He indicated that, ever since I'd stepped into my calling by 'passing over' the True Cornerstone, the accuser of the brethren had been scouring my life, looking for legal ways to block me going further.

The enemy was worried. Really worried.

Now this is good news. As well as bad news. It's good news because obviously God will open the doorway into our destiny, despite unresolved issues in our lives. It becomes clear in this process that God is not looking for perfection, He's not looking for every last ungodly covenant gone or every false refuge razed. What is He looking for?

> 'The eyes of the Lord range throughout the earth to strengthen those whose hearts are fully committed to Him.'
>
> 2 Chronicles 16:9 NIV

He's looking for commitment to the relationship. Once we begin to recognise false refuges in our lives and decide on a scorched earth policy with respect to them, we start to demonstrate a commitment to God that brings us to the attention of the Accuser. He's got to find our remaining weak spots. So it seems that he issues orders to dredge up from our past history any false refuges we've previously had—even ones we no longer use—which might be brought up in evidence before the throne of Heaven.

You might have forgotten, but that's beside the point. When I was a teenager, I developed a habit of twirling. I don't remember quite how I discovered that spinning on the spot for several minutes could relieve my stress but somehow I did. So, whenever I was worried, disappointed, upset or unhappy, I jumped up and twirled until I felt better. I stopped this habit in my late twenties—but only for purely practical reasons. I no longer lived in a house with sufficient space to do it.

And, after a while, I forgot all about it. Decades passed.

When I was first investigating thresholds and examining the spiritual dynamics involved, I discovered the Turkish word, 'dervish' meant *threshold*. This is an extremely fraught word spiritually because it refers to the whirling dancers of the Sufi religion.[4] Now this was a deeply disturbing moment for me.

I hadn't thought of all that twirling and spinning in thirty years. But into my mind there immediately popped memories of whirling and dancing all through my teen years and into my twenties. God reminded me that there was a particular trigger as I grew older. I loved the early music of Scottish singer-songwriter, Sheila Walsh. I had one cassette that I listened to over and over: it was the live recording of a concert which included both song brackets and inspirational messages. At one point, Sheila revealed that she'd always wanted to be a prophet. Every time I got to that moment in the tape, I'd think, 'Stupid! Stupid! Do you have any idea what you're asking for?' and I'd jump up and launch into a spinning frenzy.

As I recalled this, I asked God, 'What was that about?'

'You have always resisted My call,' He said. 'This was a moment when you felt it keenly. But you sensed the spirits on the threshold who demanded a sacrifice. So, because you were always unconsciously looking for another way, a back-door strategy, you tried magic.'

'Magic?'

As I read about what the Sufis were doing by spinning, I realised that one aspect of their dance was an attempt to jump over their own shadow. This, by its nature, is impossible. And so yes, it definitely seemed to me that, without ever realising it, I was instinctively reaching for an occult solution and trying to pass over the threshold by magic.

For the next fortnight, I felt like I was covered in cold, sticky tar. I believe God allowed me to sense just a little of what that pit of magic was truly like. Just so I wouldn't ever underestimate the gravity of what I'd done with that seemingly 'innocent' activity.

Again I was blessed. God brought this issue back to mind before the Accuser could bring it up. But I've since worked with people who've had false refuges in the past which came really close to wrecking their journey into the 'pass over' which marks the start of fulfilling our destiny.

I've met quite a few people who swear blind they have never had anything to do with the occult or magic—and yet have come to realise over time that they've instinctively reached for it at a critical moment. It's no coincidence that one of the lowest levels of witchcraft is termed wishcraft.

One woman casually remarked during prayer ministry that, as she'd surrendered her false refuges, a bizarre temptation had arisen. She'd been under spiritual attack and had been repeatedly enticed to use the devil as a place of comfort. She'd always resisted, but the temptation continued, unabated and growing in strength, despite intensive prayer.

She renounced her other false refuges easily and thought renouncing the devil was going to be just as simple. But she couldn't say it. She stammered, she stumbled, she fumbled—it was if her tongue and lips wouldn't work. Suddenly a long-forgotten memory popped up—when she'd been a child and she'd been chastised by her mother, she'd pout and say, 'I'm just going to sit in the corner with the devil.' And she'd plunk herself down, stew about the way she'd been treated and keep the devil company.

She'd long forgotten this habit. But the temptation, which she thought was a spiritual attack striking randomly out of nowhere, was in fact pushing her to reactivate the very false refuge she'd never legally given up: the satan himself. Eventually I had to lead her through a statement of renunciation, getting her to repeat a single word at a time after me—because she couldn't even remember a phrase long enough to speak it out.

In some cases, a false refuge doesn't actually have to have been a habit. It can have been a one-off. Another woman had worked through all the issues she knew of and believed God was calling her across the threshold into her destiny. But on the day her business opened, she had a serious car accident, a terrible breach occurred with her family and several major clients she'd lined up all cancelled without warning.

As she went to God in prayer, asking what was going on, He said, 'You have other gods before Me.' She immediately denied it but, as she waited on Him, a deeply hidden memory surfaced. She was four years old and her aunt had taken her to visit a friend. They'd locked her in a back room to play. Hours later, she was still there and had begun to be frightened. In her desperation, she looked up and noticed a small statue on a shelf. Suddenly she knew its name and begged it to help her. Moments later, to her relief, the door opened and her aunt was there.

She hadn't thought of that statute ever again—not until the moment God brought it vividly to mind after He said to her, 'You have other gods before Me.'

It's not simply a matter of current false refuges. Talk to God and ask Him to reveal the ones you've long, long forgotten. Perhaps there was a time in your life when you calmed yourself by emptying your mind and meditating using crystal gems. Perhaps you used to head off to the kinesiologist for some relief, rather than talk to God for as long as it took. Perhaps you used a rosary to repeat prayers directed at God, rather than simply chatting with Him. Perhaps you used to cross-dress, or treat yourself to a holiday or a new hairstyle, or just simply retreat to a showcase spot where you could be a noble martyr. You suffered in silence but made sure everyone knew you were suffering in silence.

You don't have to go racking your memory, looking for these past refuges—let the Holy Spirit prompt you when He blows in that direction. Otherwise you may wind up in another counterfeit haven: that of religious scruples.

Ultimately the test produces the testimony. It not only enables us to confirm that our false refuge is gone, it confirms our commitment to God. When we pass the test, however many attempts it takes, the faith in our faithfulness is quickened.

May the Lord bring us all off from every false refuge and every vain hope! May our building be founded on 'the rock of ages'! May we... be followers of Jesus and walk even as He walked in the bond of that blessed legacy.

Francis Lear, 1837
Peace, the Perfect and Assured Portion of the Believer

4

First the Raven, Then the Dove

The more resolutions you make, the more you will break. But it does not matter how many you break, so long as you are resolute not to put off repentance when you break them, but to give yourself up to the mercy which will not despise a broken and contrite heart.

Austin Farrer, *The Consuming Presence*
in *The Brink of Mystery*

Jesus had a refuge.

Isn't that just stunning?

Sometimes we forget He was tempted and tested just as we are. There are times when we need a refuge. And so, it should really come as no surprise that there were times when Jesus did too. And His choices when it comes to a refuge naturally point us to the very things we need to have in ours.

After encountering much hostility which had culminated in an attempt to stone Him to death, Jesus left Jerusalem for a safe haven: '*They tried to seize Him, but He escaped their grasp. Then Jesus went back across the Jordan to the place where John had been baptising in the early days. There He stayed.'* (John 10:39–40 NIV)

Now the place where *'John had been baptising in the early days'* is actually identified nine chapters earlier as Bethany-beyond-the-Jordan. (John 1:28) Jesus was still in that vicinity when, several months later, He received the news that His friend Lazarus was ill. It's a place on the east bank of the Jordan River, somewhere in the present-day Hashemite Kingdom of Jordan.

Now, although there are often various and multifarious contenders for the location of just about any place Jesus stayed, prayed or was laid in the tomb, I think the site of Bethany-beyond-the-Jordan can be positively identified. The issue, in my view, is that its previous name, a very famous one, had been changed over the centuries. In former times—some eight or nine hundred years previously—it was known as the Brook Cherith. And this particular watercourse was intimately associated with the prophet Elijah.

This is, in my opinion, one reason why John the Baptist started out there. As the forerunner of the Messiah and the prophesied 'Elijah who was to come',[5] it would have been the most natural thing in the world for him to begin his ministry in the ravine where the Brook Cherith flowed. Such a choice immediately identified him with Elijah, since this locale was precisely where Elijah had gone right after commencing his prophetic ministry. Elijah's opening salvo was an announcement to Ahab, king of Samaria, that no rain would fall again in Israel until he gave the say-so. On decreeing and declaring this drought, he soon received a revelation from God to seek refuge on the far side of the Jordan. There, in his hideout at the Brook Cherith, he was able to drink from the stream and to receive, at God's direction, twice-daily food parcels dropped by some obliging ravens.

Basically Elijah headed off into a region very familiar to him—the Brook Cherith was not far from his hometown of Tishbe in Gilead. This particular area was therefore important in the past and was to become very important in the future. Some decades after Jesus' ascension, the Romans invaded Galilee and Judea, and laid siege to Jerusalem. At that time, the followers of Jesus took heed of His prophecy that the Temple would be thrown down and not one stone left upon another. When He'd announced this, He'd also told His disciples to flee to the mountains and to pray that their flight would not be in winter or on the Sabbath.

So, as the Romans advanced, many Christians looked to Jesus' words and tried to work out what 'mountains' He'd referred to. They fled across the River Jordan to a city called Pella. This choice of safe haven is a mystery for many historians—it just seems so weird. Why Pella, of all places? It has no apparent significance and, as a result, some experts even doubt that it has been correctly identified in the historical record.

However, I think the matter is easily explained. Pella was the closest reasonably sized town to the Brook Cherith.

In addition, it was perched on foothills just to the west of the mountains of Gilead.[6] Furthermore it qualifies as the famous 'Refuge in Edom' predicted by Daniel in his end-times vision. Daniel prophesied that, when the King of the North invades the 'Beautiful Land' of Israel, *'These shall be delivered out of his hand: Edom and Moab and the main part of the Ammonites.'* (Daniel 11:41 ESV) In fact, while this verse speaks of what is classed by scholars as the 'Refuge in Edom', it's clear the place of deliverance is not restricted to Edom. It could also be Moab or Ammon. The Brook Cherith certainly meets that criteria because it was indeed in the ancient territory of the Ammonites.

So, if I were a first century Christian looking for a secure refuge in a time of tribulation, it would surely occur to me: the Brook Cherith is in the very same region prophesied by Daniel as a safe refuge. Furthermore it was good enough for Elijah *and* good enough for John the Baptist *and* good enough for Jesus too. Four ticks of approval. So what makes me think I could rustle up a better option?

Yet: why such an out-of-the-way place as the Brook Cherith at all? What is its significance? It's only mentioned twice in Scripture, both times in reference to the place Elijah went to escape from the wrath of Ahab and his wife, Jezebel.

Cherith—or Kerith, as it is sometimes written—means *cut*. It is associated with the cutting of a covenant.

This describes the ultimate hiding place: within the cut of a covenant. All very well to state, but what exactly does this mean? How does it work in practice? It's unrealistic for every Christian to pull up stakes and move to a wadi in Jordan. So what does this natural example tell us about the spiritual?

First of all, let's look at what happens over the centuries at the Brook Cherith.

At the beginning of his ministry, Elijah went there to hide from Ahab and was fed by some ravens. He left when the brook dried up.

At the beginning of his ministry, John the cousin of Jesus, the promised and prophesied second Elijah, preached a baptism of repentance there. Later he moved to Aenon on the western bank of the Jordan River—perhaps because the brook dried up, just as it had in the time of Elijah the Tishbite. That possibility is implied by the comment in John 3:23 that Aenon was chosen because there was plenty of water there.

Now, just prior to the beginning of His ministry, Jesus was baptised in the Brook Cherith. It was here that the Holy Spirit descended on Him like a dove. A couple of years later, just after the time of the Feast of Hanukkah, Jesus returned to the Brook Cherith. Like Elijah of old, He was hiding out from a power elite who was trying to kill Him. He stayed there throughout winter season until such time as He received news that Lazarus was deathly sick. Even then He delayed two days before leaving Bethany-beyond-the-Jordan and setting out for Bethany near Jerusalem. Is there some significance to the fact He moves from one Bethany—'house of affliction'—to another? It was an unquestionably dangerous decision to return to the environs of Jerusalem.

Thomas even realised it might well prove fatal. The disciple who has become famous throughout the history of the church for his doubts had another side to his character. He actually showed his immense bravery and loyalty at this point by encouraging his fellow-disciples to accompany Jesus: *'Let us also go, that we may die with Him.'* (John 11:16 NIV)

Jesus did not in fact return to Bethany-beyond-the-Jordan after raising Lazarus from the dead. Instead He holed up in Ephraim—another place difficult to identify. It may be a village not far from Jerusalem, but the immediate environs of the capital were very dangerous. The other possibility is 'Mount Ephraim', and if John meant that, then he was merely saying Jesus went back to Shechem. In other words, He simply returned to visit the same Samaritans who had welcomed Him previously on being evangelised by the woman who'd met Him at Jacob's Well.[7] Shechem was not only one of the designated 'cities of refuge' of ancient times but it had a long tradition of being a place where covenants were reaffirmed. That tradition went right back through Joshua, Joseph and Jacob to the time when Abram built the first of seven altars in Canaan, under a terebinth tree. So, if Mount Ephraim is where Jesus went, He simply took refuge once again in a place symbolic of a covenant cut.

The cleft of covenant is the place of being hidden from

danger. If we look back through the pages of Scripture, the motif of being hidden in the cleft of the Rock recurs time and again. Elijah not only hides from Ahab in the cleft of Cherith, the waters of covenant, but later hides from Jezebel in the cleft of Horeb, the mountain of covenant. Moses too is on that same mountain of covenant—though he called it Sinai—and he was hidden in a cleft in the Rock when the glory of the Lord passes by. He may not have been hiding from enemies but he was there, protected from danger.

Samson went to hide from the Philistines in a cleft in the rock of Etam (Judges 15:8). Jeremiah hid a linen belt in a cleft in the rock at Perath (Jeremiah 13:7) as a demonstration that, because the people of Judah had covenanted with idols, they would be ruined wherever they hid. Yet Jeremiah later exhorts the people of Moab to flee from their cities and, like the dove, make a nest in the clefts of the rock (Jeremiah 48:28).

Solomon speaks of his betrothed as a dove hiding in the cleft of a rock (Song of Solomon 2:14). This is a prophetic image of the Bride of Christ. Our one and only true and safe refuge is within the Rock—Christ Himself. We are invited to be hidden from the Enemy in the cleft, the cut, in His side.

When Nicodemus went to visit Jesus by night, he was told:

> 'No one can see the kingdom of God unless he is born again.'

> 'How can a man be born when he is old?'

Nicodemus asked. 'Can he enter his mother's womb a second time to be born?'

Jesus answered, 'Truly, truly, I tell you, no one can enter the kingdom of God unless he is born of water and the Spirit. Flesh is born of flesh, but spirit is born of the Spirit. Do not be amazed that I said, 'You must be born again.' The wind blows where it wishes. You hear its sound, but you do not know where it comes from or where it is going. So it is with everyone born of the Spirit.'

'How can this be?' Nicodemus asked.

John 3:3–9 NIV

It may not be obvious but that final question posed by Nicodemus, 'How can this be?' is ultimately the very same question as: 'How can we hide in the cleft of the Rock?'

John's gospel is not only a treasure trail of clues but a poetic masterpiece. It's constructed using a classical Hebrew design of mirror elements in reverse order. This formulation is technically called 'chiasmus'.[8] As a consequence of this poetic patterning John doesn't always present his stories about Jesus in chronological order. Rather he couples thematic sequences together. As a result, his gospel is composed of matching scenes—one to be found at the beginning and one at the end. These scenes not only inform each other but they also inform—and are informed by—adjacent scenes.

So to understand what's really being revealed in the

first episode with Nicodemus where the conversation about being born again occurs, we have to examine the matching episode where Nicodemus appears at the end. He comes in, at the crucifixion, helping Joseph of Arimathea to place Jesus in a tomb. It's implied that, along with John and the three Marys—Mary, the mother of Jesus, as well as Mary Magdalene and Mary the wife of Clopas—that he was there for Jesus' final words. That means he would have been a witness to the moment when Jesus said, '*It is finished*,' and gave up His spirit. In addition, he would have been an onlooker when one of the Roman soldiers took up a lance and pierced Jesus' side with it. He would have seen the blood and water flowing out.

Now the Greek word for 'blood' is also the word for 'spirit'. Perhaps as Nicodemus observed this, his mind returned to the words of Jesus: '*No one can enter the kingdom of God unless he is born of water and the Spirit.*'

Natural birth comes with the breaking of waters and the coming of blood. Nicodemus would have realised that, even as he watched the spear enter Jesus' side, and blood and water gushed forth, he was watching a parallel to a physical birth. And that somehow, in a strange melding, this was also a spiritual birth. The water and the 'spirit' testified to that.

I don't have any doubt that Nicodemus was baffled beyond measure. If he realised he was witnessing the new birth Jesus had spoken to him about, it must have blown his mind. Jesus had just died to bring about this unearthly birth, this birth from above, and make it available to all people. But—and it would have been a huge 'but' for Nicodemus—even putting aside the birth coming out of death aspect, whoever heard of anyone ever being born through the pierced side of a man?

Now Nicodemus was, just as Jesus had said, one of the great teachers of the law in contemporary Judea. Sometime on that terrible afternoon on the day before the Passover, a frisson of wonder must have turned his world upside down. The truth shot through his mind like a lightning discharge. Yes, there was indeed a moment in history— just one single solitary occasion—when someone had been born through the pierced side of a man. Eve, the bride of Adam, had been drawn from his side, out from under his heart.

The pieces of the prophetic jigsaw must have all come together in a rush as Nicodemus recalled the last words of Jesus: '*It is finished.*' In Hebrew, this is 'kallah' and it has another meaning. Besides *it is finished*, 'kallah' means *my bride.*[9] It is the cry of the Bridegroom signifying the consummation of a marriage.

Now we can be sure Nicodemus understood all this because of his reaction. He brought a hundred *litra* of myrrh to the tomb of Jesus. Myrrh is the 'oil of joy', and in those days it was used at the time of consummation of a marriage. Nicodemus obviously realised that a wedding needed to be celebrated: the Messiah was the second Adam who had just given birth to His bride. The chances of him having a hundred *litra* of myrrh in storage for just such an occasion are next to nil. Just a week before, Mary Magdalene[10] had been scathingly criticised for her lavish and wasteful extravagance in anointing Jesus with just one *litra* from her alabaster box. How much more profligate is a hundred *litra*? Nicodemus must have sent out servants or friends to scour every oil shop in Jerusalem for the required amount. After all, as Arie Uittenbogaard points out, he was organising the festivities for the wedding of God to all mankind.[11]

Nicodemus had stepped up to fill the gap left by John the Baptist. He was fulfilling a spectacular calling: to be the friend of the Bridegroom. To confirm this is how this final scene with Nicodemus should be interpreted, we need to look back into the chiasmus for the mirror scene. In addition, it is helpful to look at adjacent scenes as well.

Now the mirror scene to Jesus' death on the Cross happens to be the testimony of John the Baptist that Jesus is the Bridegroom. *'The bride belongs to the bridegroom. The friend who attends the bridegroom waits and listens for him, and is full of joy when he hears the bridegroom's voice. That joy is mine, and it is now complete.'* (John 3:29 NIV)

With that last word 'complete', we find an echo of Jesus' declaration: *'It is finished!'*

The adjacent scene to the crucifixion, after Nicodemus and Joseph of Arimathea lay the body of Jesus in the tomb, is of course the Resurrection. When Jesus meets Mary in the garden, their dialogue reflects that of the wedding in the Song of Songs. Jesus, son of David, uses the prophetic language of Solomon, son of David, to confirm His betrothal to His bride, the church, as it was represented by Mary Magdalene.

Their dialogue also reflects and reverses that of the Garden of Eden. In Eden, God the gardener comes looking for mankind, calling, 'Where are you?' In the garden outside the tomb, a representative of mankind, comes looking for God, calling, 'Where is He?'

Mary Magdalene not only represented humanity, she represented the Bride of Christ, taken from His side—just as Eve had been drawn from Adam.

The new birth is thus through the wound in the side of Jesus. And the covenant cut is also the wound in the side of Jesus.

When we enter by faith into that wound, we are not only born again but we are hidden from power of the Enemy.

This is the true Refuge, the cleft in the Rock, the hiding place within the Cornerstone, the covering close to God's heart, the shelter beneath the shadow of His wings, the snug nest under His prayer shawl.

So let me ask some hard, hard questions. Do you think that a prayer asking Jesus into your heart is the same as accepting His invitation to enter by faith into that wound in His side? Do you believe being christened as a baby is the same as giving your consent to His proposal to become part of His Body and His Bride? Do you think living a good life is the same as agreeing to the covenant of defence He offers, which includes a safe haven and a secure refuge?

From time to time, I get a desperate plea for help from someone whose life has become a disaster zone. They haven't picked themselves up from one barrage before the next round of carpet bombing bursts in on them from an entirely different direction. Shell-shocked, they've gone to their pastor and asked, 'Why aren't I hidden in Christ?'

The answer they've always received is along these lines: 'But you *are* hidden in Christ. You must have faith and stand on that truth.'

Faith is not being blind to reality. When the evidence that we are *not* hidden is stark and unmistakeable and is staring us directly in the face, when it's clear the enemy can attack us at will, we need to go to God and ask why.

Is it because we're acquainted with Jesus but we don't actually have a covenant with Him?

- Is it because we've got a covenant with Him but we've moved out from under its protective covering?

- Is it because, when we came to a point of testing, we dived straight into a false refuge instead of running to Jesus?

- Is it because, within the comfort of that counterfeit haven, we enjoyed the company of our idols?

- Is it because we thereby covenanted with spirits other than the Holy Spirit?

- Is it because, although we haven't personally covenanted with an ungodly spirit, we have been complicit with covenants taken out by our ancestors?

- Is it because we have directly covenanted with the goddesses or godlings of the nations by, for example, stepping over the threshold into a temple?

- Is it because we haven't repented of our actions— either because we didn't realise they actually were that serious or because we think they're all 'under the Blood'?

- Is it because we haven't revoked the covenants we've inadvertently—or even deliberately—made?

Any of these possibilities may be a major contributing factor in any situation where we find every available shred of evidence points to the fact we are not hidden in Christ. The assumption that believers are always protected is based on a misunderstanding of the theological truth that God will never break covenant with us. That is absolutely true—but it ignores the repeated teaching about Christians falling into the 'error of Balaam' which is mentioned by John, Jude and Peter.

Balaam was the diviner, hired by the king of Moab, to curse the Israelites when they were on the verge of entering into the Promised Land. The king gave Balaam three chances to speak maledictions over the tribes of Israel but, all three times, he spoke benedictions instead. He explained to the king that he could not curse when God had commanded him to bless. If you're wondering why his head was still connected to his body after saying that, it was because he gave the king a strategy. Explaining that God would never break covenant with His people, Balaam advised the king of Moab to get the people to break covenant with God. Entice them, lure them, tempt them to covenant—to *become one*—with one of the Baals and thus to abandon their covenant with God.

The tactic worked brilliantly. The king rounded up some beautiful high-class priestesses of Baal Peor, *the lord of the opening*, and sent them to the Israelite camp to beguile the men into ritual prostitution. In ritual prostitution, as in eating food sacrificed to idols, the purpose of the ceremony is to 'become one with the god'. This was not only covenant, it was a complete betrayal of Yahweh. This is why sexual immorality, as well as eating food sacrificed to idols or that had been strangled or had blood still in it, were the sole restrictions placed on Gentiles converting to Christianity. The council of Jerusalem under the leadership of Peter settled the question of whether the Gentiles needed to be circumcised, and show in their body the sign of covenant, in the negative—but with the proviso that the Gentiles not do things that would bring them into oneness with another spirit and thus take them out from under the covenantal protection of the Lord.

This is a general principle, not a comprehensive list.

Today, we might also add such things as:

- touring   foreign   temples—because   stepping

through a doorway, guarded by spirits, is accepting the hospitality of a threshold covenant; and it not only makes it worse if we curse the deity within, but also brings us into violation of God's instructions in Jude 1:8–11 and 2 Peter 2:10–17, both of which mention the error of Balaam.

- practising yoga—which means 'yoke'; it is an exercise routine which, in a counterfeit of the easy yoke and light burden of Jesus, 'yokes' us into oneness with a spirit worshipped within the Hindu religion, the kundalini spirit, better known within the pages of Scripture as the spirit of Python.

- 'trading'. This involves investing money on a spiritual trading floor—sometimes declared to be the heavenly 'sea of glass' and therefore a clean platform to conduct business with God—with the expectation that God will grant favour in a specific area.[12]

Trading and covenant are so often confused in the literature that it's worth making a careful distinction between them. Covenant involves oneness and unity, however trading involves distinctness and isolation.

Trading involves exchange for mutual benefit. It is about a commercial transaction.

Covenant involves exchange for mutual affection. It is about relational intimacy.

Trading involves the bartering of a portion of your goods or your time with an expectation of profit.

Covenant involves gifting of everything you are—the totality of your being—and/or the gifting of everything you have—the totality of your possessions—to someone with whom your heart has been united. Covenant means vulnerability, transparency, utter and complete surrender to another person.

Trading may involve bartering, haggling, negotiating for a better deal.

Covenant has only one price and it's non-negotiable: all in exchange for all, everything in exchange for everything.

God asks us to consecrate ourselves to Him in covenant. So intense is this consecration, this oneness with Him and with no other, that eventually He will start to talk to us about the covenant over our names. Our identity is encoded in our names and to dedicate our everything to Him, including our identity, our names need a massive overhaul.[13]

But this overhaul is not even remotely possible unless we first deal with our false refuges by beginning the work of repentance.

When Jesus went to the Brook Cherith and was baptised by John, the Holy Spirit descended on Him like a dove.

Long centuries before, the prophet Elijah had been fed here by ravens.

Both ravens and doves are symbols associated with baptism. The dove might be obvious, the raven less so.

In the ark a few people, only eight souls, were saved

through water. And this water symbolises the baptism that now saves you—not the removal of dirt from the body, but the pledge of a clear conscience toward God. It saves you through the resurrection of Jesus Christ.

1 Peter 3:20–21 BSB

The water of the Flood, according to Peter, symbolises baptism. So what do the raven and the dove symbolise, both in terms of the receding of the waters, as well as location where Jesus was baptised?

The dove, of course, makes us think of the Holy Spirit, of peace and purity. It is a 'clean' bird. It's said that a dove won't come into land if its nest is out of order. Brian Simmons footnotes John 1:32 in the Passion Translation with this thought:

> *Jesus, the Lamb, took away our sins, and the Holy Spirit, the Dove, brings to man the life of God. Jesus didn't come to start a movement but to bring the fullness of life to us. This 'Dove' points to the dove that Noah released from the ark. It found no place to rest in a fallen world. The last time Noah released the dove it flew and never returned. It flew throughout history over Abraham and the patriarchs, over the prophets and kings with no place to rest, until at last, there was a heavenly man who carried the life of heaven—upon him the dove (Holy Spirit) rested and remained. There was nothing that could offend heaven in the life of our Lord Jesus.*

But what of the raven? What does it signify? A raven is a scavenger, eating dead flesh, and thus an 'unclean' bird. In Hebrew, its name is 'oreb', from a root for *evening* or *to become dark.* Its feathers are a deep, glossy black, in contrast to the pristine white or soft, muted grey of the dove. It is associated in some cultures with prophecy, divination and death. Many believers instinctively associate the raven-dove symbolism with the flesh-spirit contrast or with the old man-new man transformation.

And while that is one interpretation and a very valid one, I am inclined to think that the raven and the dove are symbols of Jesus and the Holy Spirit. When Noah released the raven, it did not return. It didn't need to. There was plenty of death around for it to feed on. A raven symbolises a death-eater: and this too is what Jesus did. He took our sins on Himself, with all the uncleanness and defilement that entailed. He was the One who swallowed up death in victory. (1 Corinthians 15:54)

His invitation to covenant is one to eternal life: to allow Him to apply His defeat of death to our lives.

We not only have to give up our false refuges, we have to stop exalting them as the answer to loneliness, rejection, anxiety, distress, misery:

> *Music was my refuge. I could crawl into the space between the notes and curl my back to loneliness.*
>
> Maya Angelou

I take refuge in my books.

Julia Ward Howe

Each positive thought is your refuge and your sanctuary, where in that thoughtful moment, you are safe.

Bryant McGill

Life is a love story, with every character yearning for permanent refuge in someone's heart.

Richelle E. Goodrich

There are three means of refuge from the challenges of life; good music, good friends and good food.

Natasha Potter

Music, friends, food, books, thoughts, another's heart: all these are ultimately false refuges. Elisabeth Elliot puts us on the right track:

Where does your security lie? Is God your refuge, your hiding place, your stronghold, your shepherd, your counsellor, your friend, your redeemer, your saviour, your guide? If He is, you don't need to search any further for security.

But it is medieval author, Thomas à Kempis, *the little hammer,*[14] who nailed the matter most succinctly in *The Inner Life*:

Let all your thoughts be with the Most High, and direct your humble prayers unceasingly to Christ. If you cannot contemplate high and heavenly things, take refuge in the Passion of Christ, and love to dwell within His Sacred Wounds. For if you devoutly seek the Wounds of Jesus and the precious marks of His Passion, you will find great strength in all troubles.

5

The Limitations of Repentance

My heart and my mouth are full of a God who cannot be localized, mastered or conjured with. In a sense, he stays put, for he is the Rock: but just because of his granite-like consistency he overrides and changes all the means and methods of his presence. Because his purpose stands, they cannot stand; for his purpose needs variety of fulfillment in the various stages of his work. He taught Solomon to build a temple, he caused Nebuchadnezzar to sweep it away. Old things pass; he makes them continually new.

Austin Farrer, *Idols*
in *The Brink of Mystery*

Almost anything can be turned into a false refuge. And it's not even blatantly obvious sin that is most insidious, but rather subtle habits that can actually seem godly. Prayer—yes, of all things, *prayer*—can be a false refuge if we focus on the prayer itself, rather than the Lord who answers it. When we've got to go get the right person with the right anointing to intercede for us, or speak the right words in the right order or attain the right level of faith, we should question where our heart is inclined. Are we picking up the phone to ask for prayer, rather than stepping before the throne of grace? Are we looking to the method or to the Messiah?

John Loren Sandford said that human beings are inveterate idol-makers. Once you begin to topple your false refuges, you'll discover how true that is. As idol-makers, we are continually tempted to the formula for getting back to God, rather than simply asking Him where the relationship has gone wrong.

This leads us into directing people towards things, rather than Jesus. Jackie Hill Perry points out:

> God isn't calling gay people to be straight. You'd think He was by listening to the ways Christians try to encourage same-sex-attracted people within, or outside, their local churches. They dangle the possibility of heterosexual marriage above their heads, point to it like it's heaven on a string, something to grab and get whole with. And though it's usually well-meaning it's very dangerous. Why? Because it puts more emphasis on marriage as the goal of the Christian life than knowing Jesus.
>
> As Jeff Vanderstelt stated so well, 'The gospel doesn't just bring about forgiveness of sins and save us from hell. The gospel of Jesus Christ empowers us to live a whole new life by the same Spirit who raised Jesus from the dead.'[15]

This is what grace is: the empowerment to live the impossible commandments of Jesus. Moses only said,

'Don't kill,' but Jesus raised the bar to an unattainable height with: 'Don't even get angry—that's murder in the heart.' Moses only said, 'Don't commit adultery,' but Jesus raised the bar to another unattainable height with: 'Don't even look lustfully at another—that's adultery of the heart.' Moses only said, 'Don't steal,' but Jesus pushed the bar to the other side of the galaxy with: 'Give all you have to the poor and come follow Me.'

Grace is used in two different senses in the gospels and epistles. One meaning is God's unmerited and undeserved favour towards the world He loves and wants to redeem. The second meaning is God's empowerment to overcome sin and obey His commands.

Once we realise how deep the sin problem is and how automatic our propensity to create a false refuge out of anything to hand, we will eventually recognise that repentance is actually a gift of grace. Repentance doesn't actually work, unless God by His grace empowers it. In fact, forgiveness doesn't actually work either, unless God by His grace empowers it. John Loren Sandford points out that we don't forgive—God accomplishes forgiveness within us.

I was once asked: 'Can depression be a false refuge?' At first I thought it was unlikely. However, when the man asking the question revealed he only got depressed when he'd made up his mind he was going to come into God's calling for him, I changed my mind. Once I'd talked with him on a few more occasions, I realised just what the call on his life was. It was so stupendous that he couldn't face it—and, rather than tackle the giants, he used depression as a coping mechanism. However, inevitably that would sink into suicidal thoughts. He couldn't give up his false refuge until he accepted God's call on his life.

And sometimes this is the issue. It's not that we're disappointed or disillusioned, it's that we're scared. What God is asking us to do is too big for us. Well, of course it is. If it wasn't then we'd do it in our own strength not His.

> *God has given us both His promise and His oath. These two things are unchangeable because it is impossible for God to lie. Therefore, we who have fled to Him for refuge can take new courage, for we can hold on to His promise with confidence.*
>
> Hebrews 6:18 NLT

When God is not our first thought, He becomes our last resort. And that's how it becomes so easy for us to create false refuges—through simple habits of seeking God somewhere other than first. Those habits are as varied as humanity itself. Some people use anger as a refuge, some use withdrawal. Some people become bullies, others befriend a bully so he becomes their protector. Some people use cigarettes to soothe their moods, some people treat themselves with gourmet dining, some people gossip. Some people use their imagination to confect a fantasy—this includes adventure fantasy in which they feature as the hero of their own story, as well as sexual fantasy, or just simply internally revising or rewriting history until they are the innocent party in a dispute. Gardening and cleaning, even going to Christian conferences or the

Courts of Heaven can be ways of avoiding God.

So many of us believe we're hiding in God's protective shadow when actually our ever-present help in time of trouble is a packet of cheese biscuits. Or a favourite show on Netflix. Or a spin in the car. Or a beer. Or two.

And then there's sport. Both playing and watching. But mostly the latter. In fact, watching sport is such a common false refuge that we fail to notice the in-your-face idols associated with it. All false refuges involve idols but in sport, they aren't subtle. They are screamingly obvious. So often we invest both emotionally and financially in talismans—mascots and good luck charms. The word 'mascot' in fact is believed to come from a provincial French word for a *sorceror's amulet, a faerie friend* or *an object to bring good fortune*. In addition, the team spirit evident in sports fans is akin to counterfeit covenant. And for many people, even believers, the time they give to watching sport in one day vastly outweighs the time they spend with God in a week or even a month.

Now there's nothing wrong with watching sport, eating cheese biscuits, taking a spin in the car, streaming a show on Netflix or drinking a beer. Just so long as none of them substitute for God.

Having given due warning previously to beware of any formulaic approach, I can nevertheless say there are guidelines we can use.

Experienced counsellor Gloria Roberts indicates we should break the power of any agreement we have with the enemy. This includes vows, lies and pacts. She advocates saying aloud:

'I resign as the protector of my life.'

'I ask for a mantle of protection from You, Jesus.'

'Holy Spirit, show me any remaining vows.'

Now, I would add to this: have a witness. Raising a covenant is not, by its nature, a solitary event—so too, beginning the process of eliminating one should not be solitary either. Our postmodern culture might celebrate rugged individualism but God asks us to gather as His Body. Furthermore, the dismantling of a false refuge is a step in commitment to God—why spoil it by ignoring His desire to have two or three praying in His name? Unless, of course, rugged individualism is another undetected false refuge.

So I would also add to Gloria's prayers: 'Lord, show me any dormant refuges.'

She points out that the spirit of heroin says: 'I am your friend.' However, there are other spirits that say that too. In fact, they say: 'I am your *only* friend.'

Most subtle amongst them, in my view, are the spirits of forgetting and rejection. They are allies as well as threshold guardians—and their purpose in acting as watchers is to stop us passing over into our life's calling. As we approach the threshold that will mean entering into the purposes for which God created us, one or both of them will test us. Or perhaps we might find ourselves confronted with one of their friends amongst the fiends: Python, the spirit of constriction, Rachab, the spirit of wasting, Leviathan, the spirit of backlash, as well as the spirit of armies or a vampire spirit.

They want us to make a sacrifice to them and thus covenant with them. If they fail in that, they want us to go lick our wounds in a false refuge—meaning, while we may not be covenanting with them, at least we're making an idol of something or someone, other than the Most High God. Our idol could be cigarettes or the adrenaline rush of extreme sports, it could be freemasonry or masturbation, it could be books or cooking.

However, there is an ideal idol as far as these spirits are concerned. The spirit of forgetting will try to drive you into the clutches of the spirit of rejection so you will panic and react thoughtlessly, perhaps even irrationally. These spirits want you to *wish*, rather than *pray*.

Some of my false refuges were simple to crush. Coffee. Twirling. Taking long baths.

But eventually there arose a life situation where God took the opportunity to reveal another false refuge. It is tough. So tough. And I say, 'is' because it's present and ongoing and, although God has graciously given me many tests—and by *many*, I mean hundreds—I simply haven't passed them in any definitive way.

My as-yet-undefeated-at-the-time-of-writing false refuge is mental rehearsal. Every time someone does something unjust to me or to someone I care about, I prepare speeches in my mind. I carefully craft exactly what I'm going to say next time I see the perpetrator. I polish my phrases, I make sure they perfectly express the nature of the injustice— and then, because I realise that the conversation might not go the way it's come out in my head, I start again. Scenario after scenario goes through my thoughts. Tiny divergences in the flow of the conversation are planned for. The relentless mental rehearsal for all possibilities goes on so I can ensure the perpetrator will receive the best possible piece of my mind.

Perhaps you're thinking to yourself as I confess this: 'Anne, you do not have a clue about the demons that haunt my life. All your false refuges are so trivial by comparison.' To which I say this: comparison is irrelevant. There is no such thing as a good false refuge. Don't mistake sin for what it is just because it's wearing a socially acceptable mask.

Mental rehearsal. As soon as God pointed it out to me, I knew I was in deep trouble. I went to Him and I said, 'Coffee was nothing compared to this. I don't think I can do it. In fact, I'm sure I *can't* do it. It's really fortunate You forgive people seventy times seven each day, because I think I'm going to be using every single one of those opportunities.'

And to start with, I did. I'd catch myself a few seconds into preparing a speech and I'd take it to God. But those old, rutted tracks were so smooth and slippery that sometimes I'd be several minutes into the mental rehearsal before I became aware of it. And there were the days when I just didn't want to go to God. I *wanted*, I *desired*, I felt the siren lure of the comfort promised by expressing my anger this way.

I had to go to God and say, 'At one level, I totally believe that the atonement is all-sufficient to get me through this. But there's a part of me fighting that with all my might. I know that the atonement can overcome my unbelief but I need You to do it. Because I can't.'

Why is this the hard one? There are a couple of reasons: one, this is the false refuge that, for me, is most profoundly linked to rejection. Two, there are limitations to repentance and I was about to hit that wall.

Remember I quoted John Loren Sandford's remark that human beings are inveterate idol-makers? Yes, we can even make *repentance* into a false refuge.

Repentance is a gift of God. It's a grace gift. It doesn't have any power in and of itself to transform our lives. God, by His sovereign grace, just happens to allow it to work that way. Until the day that He puts a stop on His permission.

Sooner or later, that day will come. It will come when we begin to rely on the gift, instead of the Giver. Because when that time arrives, it means we've already started to work out our salvation in fear and trembling plus our own strength. Repentance has defaulted to formula. At that point it can no longer be what it is meant to be: a component in the restoration of relationship.

It's often a perplexing time for believers: they don't understand what's gone wrong. Repentance has always worked in the past. For some, it's worked for decades.

They know its power; they are well-acquainted with the efficacy of the Blood of Jesus and the authority of the Cross to remove sin. But suddenly... without warning... there's nothing. They turn on the motor and the reliable, faithful, never-had-a-day's-problem-with-it car doesn't start. So, they look for why: hidden sin must be the answer. They scour their souls, repenting and re-repenting of everything they can think of. All they can find is minor, almost trivial stuff, but maybe it's enough to cause the blockage. They forgive and re-forgive, just in case they lacked authenticity the first time.

But the fact is: now we're down to the wire in our relationship with God. The Hound of Heaven knows we're committed to Him but will we leap the final wall that is heaven-high and hell-deep? And that final wall is painted in letters tall and wide: *unbelief in the atonement.*

Lisa Gungor, once described as 'Christian music royalty', released a YouTube video describing her total loss of faith in God. She said this: 'My whole perspective on faith has been a transaction. *If I'm good enough, if I pray enough, if I believe enough*, then I get blessings... You have to conform in the church. If you have doubts, you're a dangerous person.'

If... if... if... As I listened to Lisa, I couldn't help but hear in those instances of 'if', the calling card of the spirit of Python. The temptation was clearly tailor-made to Lisa's circumstances: 'You only get out what you put in.' As I listened I recognised all the usual suspects when it comes to our subtle attempts at manipulation of God: expecting to have to perform for His approval; giving to Him in order to get from Him rather than giving to express our love.

Without pointing any fingers at Lisa—because let me say this is true of all of us—her problem comes down to unbelief in the atonement.

What exactly does that mean? The atonement, the at-one-ment, is the covenantal oneness which was lost in Eden and which Jesus restored to us through His death on the cross.[16] We can't credit that the wounds of Jesus are actually the passageway into the new birth and that nothing else is needed.

This is the soul of darkness for all of us. This is why, even as believers, we are disquieted by the searing Light who dazzles us with His beauty and love. Surely there's something we can add to the all-sufficient sacrifice of Jesus? What can we do to help God save us? Be good? Obey the commandments? Sow a seed of faith? Trade on the sea of glass? Forgive? Repent?

Fundamentally all of these are 'doing' things. Our desire to 'do'—something, anything—that will make a difference to God's response, even hastening its arrival, is like a battering ram pounding away at the walls of our lives. The cry of our heart for God to move on our behalf becomes increasingly desperate and impatient.

This is a story as old as Abram. God covenanted with him, promising to make him the father of a great nation, even though he didn't have a son. Several months down the track Sarai decided to help God out by suggesting Abram father a child through her maid-servant Hagar. Abram agreed.

But fourteen years after this, God's timing finally arrived and Sarah gave birth to a son, Isaac. But her inability to truly trust God had devastating consequences—consequences that persist down the millennia to the present day. The cauldron of rage in the Middle East boils down to a conflict between her descendents and those of Hagar.

We have to come to the point of realising that our 'doing', however well-motivated, however holy in appearance, however chapter-and-verse sanctioned, does nothing for God. We 'do' simply because He asks for it. We respond in love—and it's a tawdry, self-interested love, make no mistake, but He's willing to accept what we've got—simply by 'doing' what He asks.

Part of our heart wants to do deals with God. It wants the transactional Christianity Lisa Gungor talks about. The whole 'grace thing' is too scary. It puts all the control in God's hands and none in ours. And, for those of us who need to be in control, that's a terrifying prospect.

Now while repentance doesn't do the slightest thing— it doesn't add to the atonement of Jesus in any way— that doesn't mean to say we should not repent of our false refuges. God asks it of us. That's the reason we should do it—out of our commitment to relationship with Him. Yet it's not going to make Him love us more or give us a heavenly gold star of approval or reward us with higher favour.

Forgiveness doesn't do the slightest thing either. The reason forgiveness and repentance are so transformative in our lives is not because they give us any big tick of divine endorsement to trade with for His favour, but simply because of God's waterfall of grace into our lives.

When we repent of our false refuges, when we renounce our vows and surrender our idols, God's grace flows—restoring, sometimes initiating covenant in our lives. We begin to come into oneness with Him.

Hear me well and hear me carefully at this point. Because I'm at the limits of language and may trip over my own words in the paradox of this situation. We can't 'do' anything to enhance the atonement of Jesus; yet we are asked to 'do' repentance and 'do' forgiveness in order to come into the oneness God desires to have with us. We are asked to 'do' surrender and make a total offering of self. And at the same time we are asked to recognise that all of this 'doing' is ineffective. Even this surrender is only made possible by the power of the Cross and the atonement of Jesus. He does it all.

All.

All.

All.

In addition this surrender is a day-by-day thing. Every time I start to grind my teeth and find myself mentally rehearsing the piece of my mind that I'm going to present to the offender next time I see him, I have to take the thought captive and take myself off to chat with God. 'It's me again. I'm sorry again. Actually that apology was more of a reflex than anything because I'm not feeling especially sorry. You know, Lord, I'd love to release the tension I feel by letting myself finish the speech I've started. I don't even want to talk to You about this. I need Your grace and the power of the atonement to get through this—again. I want to distract myself and turn on the radio and listen to some Christian worship music, but that would be just another subtle way of avoiding You, wouldn't it?'

Holley Gerth in *fiercehearted* encapsulates the moment we need to reach in these words:

> I suddenly asked, 'Jesus, will you be good for me?' I didn't mean 'good for me' in the way we say it about broccoli or wearing sunscreen. I meant it like, 'Will you be good in my place? In other words will you touch the rafters for me? Will you be perfect on my behalf? Will you cover over all the errors in the script of my life with the red pen that is the cross?'

> And you know what? He said yes. Because the scandalous miracle of the gospel is that He always says yes to prayers like that one, however strangely worded or timed they may be... I have been a grace-plus girl. Grace plus my efforts. Grace plus my goodness. Grace plus my trying. All those pluses only subtract from what Jesus is freely giving me. What has already been mine for so long.

And, despite the grace, every day is another battle. And

98

some battles are more intense than others. And some days have more skirmishes than others.

When I first began to speak openly about my struggles with false refuges, I discovered they were common. Rosemary wrote:

> One more false refuge that has come to my attention, that I didn't mention before because it's still unraveling, is something I have done since a child—retreat into my own head. Some would say that is just an active imagination, but it's not that. Like your twirling, my go-to escapes were the stories I could create in my head. It was wishing. More than a good imagination or just daydreaming, because part of the unraveling has been coming to an understanding of the difference between 'wishing' and imagination. It's very hard to distinguish, I think. I have renounced it, but there may be more to be revealed about it.

Surrender brings grief as well as relief. God's unconditional terms require us to hand over to Jesus the chisel we've been using on others so He can start chipping away at the stony parts of our heart which reject Him. These rock-hard ice-cold sections have a core of unbelief surrounded by an impenetrable shield of denial.

God in His grace and in His love for us doesn't demand we are perfect before He can usher us into our calling. He asks for commitment, not faultless, flawless behaviour.

And when we do commit to making Him first in our lives, when we take action in doing away with our false refuges and counterfeit havens, He will break our covenant with death. And He promises that when He breaks it, amazing things will happen.

Signs as wondrous as the sun standing still or an inland tsunami, as amazing as a shadow going back ten paces in the wrong direction. As astronomically impossible as the eclipse at the time of the death of Jesus.[17] In other words, as God Himself puts it in Isaiah 28:21, He will do a 'strange work', a 'disturbing task', an 'alien act', a 'mysterious deed' in the natural world. You'll look out, incredulous, at what you're seeing with your own eyes. Hopefully it won't be as dramatic as the world-shaking events I've described at the beginning of the paragraph—but it can be things like seeing an aurora or a 'sun dog' in the tropics, an earthquake thousands of kilometres from a fault line, a lightning bolt from a clear sky, a night rainbow.

But first, before that sign of the dissolution of the covenant with death can appear, we must carry out our part. Let it be said of us, as Paul said of the believers in Thessalonica: *'Your faith in God has become known everywhere... how you turned to God from idols to serve the living and true God.'* (1 Thessalonians 1:8–9 NIV)

To turn from idols, we have to give up our false refuges. Often we don't even realise we have idols because the legitimate gifts of God have been used by opportunistic spirits to create such a comfortable prison for us that we prefer it to freedom.

Dismantling the false refuge is the first step in a long process to enable us to enter our calling. As soon as people realise they have a massive problem involving crossing the threshold into their calling, they want to know what will solve the issue.

Yet, as I've pointed out throughout this book, there is no easy fix.

Well, actually, there is an easy fix—and it's called 'relationship with God'. However that's not exactly the simple whizz-bang click-your-fingers and say-this-special-prayer solution most people are looking for.

To begin this pilgrimage back to God, to find the true refuge that is within the covenant cut, we have to come out of denial and into a place of recognition. We need to recognise that we would be hidden in Christ and that we wouldn't have a problem *if* God really is our hiding place in trouble, our haven in crisis, our run-to Dad when life has disappointed us and things have gone terribly, terribly wrong.

So many people declare the words of Psalm 91, often even daily, not recognising its conditional nature:

> *If you say, "The Lord is my refuge," and you make the Most High your dwelling, no harm will overtake you, no disaster will come near your tent.*

For He will command His angels concerning
you to guard you in all your ways; they will
lift you up in their hands, so that you will not
strike your foot against a stone. You will tread
on the lion and the cobra; you will trample the
great lion and the serpent.

"Because he loves Me," says the Lord, "I will rescue
him; I will protect him, for he acknowledges My
name. He will call on Me, and I will answer him;
I will be with him in trouble, I will deliver him
and honour him. With long life I will satisfy him
and show him My salvation."

Psalm 91:9–16 NIV

Notice the first word: *if*. And while it's not obvious to us, the third word here in this English translation, 'say', isn't simply a matter of speaking out or declaring. To separate words from action was never the Hebrew way of thinking; so to say, '*The Lord is my refuge*,' while having a safe harbour away from God makes the daily ritual meaningless.

The second step after recognising the false refuge is repentance. It's turning away from the unholy hiding place, giving up the secret idol, taking an axe to the counterfeit haven. So that when you declare verses like Psalm 27:5, the words will be clean and undefiled:

In the day of trouble He will keep me safe in
His dwelling; He will hide me in the shelter of
His sacred tent and set me high upon a rock.

Psalm 27:5 NIV

So, let me ask: as you've read this book and seen the different ways believers can run to a refuge other than God, what's caused you to pause? The examples I have given are by no means comprehensive, but they are representative of the different categories into which false refuges fall: mental, emotional, physical, verbal, sexual, spiritual.

Are you ready to put to death what you believe is your only way of coping?

Then here and now name your hideout from God when you're disappointed in Him. Say what you do when you need to 'lick your wounds'. Tell Him how you behave when you are in need of comfort or protection.

As you did that, you confessed. God already knew about the things you spoke of, but now you've come into agreement with Him about their deadly effect in your life. That's all confession means: *agreement*.

Now, for repentance.

Be guided by the Holy Spirit in your repentance. Pray in your own words and language, something like this:

> Father God, I hold on to the tassels of Love's cloak—the prayer shawl of Jesus, my mediator—and I ask Him to intercede for me before Your throne. You know I can't do this, but He can. You know that half of me desperately wants to repent and to be the one to take an axe to my false refuge and smash it beyond repair. You also know that the other

103

half of me wants to fortify it and decorate it with even more creature comforts.

So, Father, although I am about to say, 'I repent', it's only true if Jesus comes to empower my words through His cross, His blood and His wounds.

Father, I repent of grieving you through my unbelief and wounding Your heart.

Father, I repent of all these false refuges I have confessed and I repent of using them out of my unbelief in the atonement.

Father, I repent of ever treating your gifts of repentance, forgiveness and reconciliation at the cross of Jesus as a formula.

Father, I repent of my patchwork of belief and unbelief which leads to mockery of the atonement.

Father, I repent of allowing those stony parts of my heart to continue to refuse to accept the all-sufficiency of the sacrifice of Jesus.

Father, I acknowledge that these words I have just spoken do nothing unless the atonement of Jesus empowers them.

Father, I now ask You to direct Your angel axemen to descend and to chop down these false refuges so that they can never be rebuilt.

Father, I give You permission to command that every stronghold of my life that dishonours You is smashed so that not one stone is left upon another.

Father, I ask You to rewire my neural processes and the networks in my brain so that I can take these thoughts and habits captive and present them to You.

Father, I ask for Your love to overshadow me and Your grace to empower me as Your Spirit leads me into an ever-stronger belief in the all-sufficiency of Jesus' sacrifice for me.

Father, I will need the help of Jesus, my mediator, and of the Holy Spirit, my advocate, as I face the test that lies before me. Please send them speedily to my aid when the time comes. Please alert me as I enter the test and remind me to seek You first, foremost and always.

I thank You and bless You for making this redemption possible. I praise the name of Jesus of Nazareth. I confess Him as Lord of my life. And just as Your chosen people still tuck prayers into the crevices of the western wall in the City where You have placed Your name, so I ask Jesus to tuck me into the wound in His side and hide me from all the power of the enemy.

I declare You to be my true refuge, now and always. And I ask the Holy Spirit to prompt me to keep under cover whenever I am tempted to come out from the shelter of Your covenant.

Thank You, Father, for Your kiss that clothes me in Your armour. May Your name be praised throughout all ages.

Blessing and honour and glory and power belong to You and to the Lamb forever and ever. Amen.

Having passed the test, you come to a different place. You may need to revoke a covenant with Death—or you may find that Jesus has already done it for you. You may discover another false refuge—or you may find the Holy Spirit talking to you about a name covenant. You may realise you need deliverance—or you may finding Jesus sweeping you off your feet and carrying you across the threshold into the calling that has awaited you from before the birth of time itself.

Whatever happens, there's only one way forward—stay close to Jesus. Hide yourself, by faith, under the wings of His prayer shawl, deep in the covenant cut that lies close to His heart.

Summary

A false refuge is a place of comfort away from God. In times of disillusionment, disappointment or distress, we naturally seek solace for our souls. However, when this relief habitually comes from anywhere or anyone other than God, we created a false refuge.

The prophet Isaiah links a false refuge to a covenant with Death and also to the substitution of an idol for the worship of the true God.

Our false refuges stand between us and our ability to come into the calling and destiny God has for us.

False refuges can range from deceptively harmless and innocent to totally destructive. They fall into the following categories: mental, emotional, physical, verbal, sexual, spiritual.

Just about anything can be turned into a false refuge—switching the gift into the place reserved for the Giver.

To remove a false refuge, we need to repent of turning from God to a worthless idol.

Repentance is a gift of grace and only 'works' because of God's grace. We therefore use it until it stops 'working'—

and then we need to acknowledge that it has become a formula and thus has come to stand between us and Jesus. At this point we have come face-to-face with our own unbelief in the atoning power of the blood of Jesus.

To find true refuge is to conceal ourselves, as Jesus did, within a covenantal cut. He did so in the natural, we must do it in the spiritual. To be hidden in Christ, we must be 'born again'. The meaning of this phrase is revealed in John's gospel as entering by faith into the wound in the side of Jesus under His heart. This is the prophesied cleft in the Rock—the Rock who is Jesus and the cleft which is the nesting place and cradle of His Bride.

Endnotes

1. The specific invaders referred to by Isaiah were the Assyrians under the command of Sennacherib.

2. In *Gay Girl, Good Girl*, Jackie Hill Perry makes these insightful comments:

   'If only I could just lay aside homosexuality, God would accept me and call me His own, I used to think. This delusion was the belief that only one aspect of my life was worthy of judgment, while the rest deserved heaven. That my other vices were "not as bad." They were just struggles that I had to work on instead of repenting.

   'There is a possibility that this kind of self-righteous thinking is why salvation has eluded many same-sex-attracted men and women. You will hear them say how they've sought God's help in this matter. They have asked Him to make them straight and He has, according to them, denied them access to the miraculous. Because God did not take hold of their gay desires and replace them with straight desires, they have no other choice but to follow where their affections may lead. The error is this: they have come to God believing that only a fraction of themselves needs saving. They have therefore neglected to acknowledge the rest of them needs to be made right. It is like coming to God offering only a portion of their heart for Him to have, as if He does not have the right to take hold of it all or as if what has been withheld from Him can be satisfied without Him.

'A thorough survey of my own heart, led entirely by the Spirit, allowed me to see what I'd never seen: that I needed freedom from homosexuality, but from all sin. I was holistically in need of God.'

3. 'Yoga' means *yoked*. It refers to being yoked to the kundalini spirit which is a threshold guardian, referred to in the Scriptures as 'Python'. This spirit has the legal right to test us on the threshold into our calling, so attempting to bind it is seriously counter-productive. (For more information, see *Dealing with Python: Spirit of Constriction*, the first book in this series.)

4. If you're Australian, you may remember the dervishes from the Gallipoli-themed Russell Crowe movie, *The Water Diviner*, where the symbolism of the windmill merges with the symbolism of the whirling dancers.

5. Matthew 11:14, Matthew 17:10–12, Mark 9:11–13.

6. Paradoxically, it is 30 metres below sea level! But nevertheless it is still high above the floor of the Jordan valley. If you're going to head for the hills, it definitely qualifies—but only in a relative sense. It was in Gilead where the famous 'balm of Gilead' was sourced.

7. Since the gospel writer is John, who is the only one also mentions the incident of the woman at the well, you may ask yourself why he simply didn't say 'Sychar' once more, if 'Ephraim' is the same place. Why isn't he consistent in identifying localities? In our modern age, we value logic but the past valued poetry. And an

important consideration for John is that his gospel is in fact a vast poem, fashioned in the Hebrew manner. He uses the literary device known as chiasmus—that is, reflected ideas built around a centre. In addition, as MJJ Menken has shown (in *Numerical Literary Techniques in John: The Fourth Evangelist's Use of Numbers of Words and Syllables*), he uses a stressed syllable count as a principal architectural device in the mathematical sub-structure of various scenes. Stressed syllables are about rhythm. This means each scene is basically either a poem or a song. Thus the choice of name to identify a town would be influenced more by poetic considerations than any need for consistency. In addition, because gematria may also have been a significant aspect of the writing, then the choice of name may have been further influenced by the mathematical value of the words in Greek. These are: Ephraim (656); Shechem, spelled 'Sychem' in Greek and mentioned in Acts 7:16 (1245); Sychar (1301).

8. The following information is taken from my book, *God's Pottery*. There I look at the first eleven mirrored pairs. However there are many more. I believe the entire gospel is constructed in mirrored pairs and its central 'scene' is the statement by Jesus claiming to be the Good Shepherd and the Gate of the Sheep in John 10. I also believe that the vexed question about the validity of the story of the woman caught in adultery—which does not appear in some early manuscripts of John and is placed in Luke's gospel in others—can be readily solved because of this ring-like structure. The story of the woman does indeed belong in John's gospel but, in my view, it should be positioned at the end of chapter 8 rather than at the beginning.

The elements of the chiasmus include, but are not limited to:

1. 496 syllables at the opening and 496 words in the final scene.

2. 17 words in the first sentence and the 17th triangular number (153) mentioned in the final scene. This use of 17 is in defiance of the Greek ideal of beauty in art and literature which considered this number to be the 'antiphraxis', variously translated as *disjunction, precaution, obstruction, barrier* and *abomination.*

3. At the beginning there is the testimony of a man named John while, mirroring it at the end, is the testimony of the disciple Jesus loved—John the apostle.

4. John the Baptist's testimony is about the Lamb of God, while John the apostle's final testimony is of an incident involving himself, Simon Peter and a matter of Lambs and Sheep.

5. The five disciples listed at the beginning include Simon Peter and Nathanael and the seven disciples at the end are grouped to make five sets, which also include Simon Peter and Nathanael. These are the only times Nathanael is mentioned anywhere in Scripture.

6. The five disciples at the beginning follow Jesus to Galilee at the beginning of His ministry; the five sets of disciples follow Jesus to Galilee at His instruction, after the Resurrection.

7. At the beginning, the doubts of a disciple are mentioned; likewise at the end. The disciple at the beginning who has doubts is Nathanael and the one at the end is Thomas. This is the only occasion in the first eleven elements of the ring-structure where the names do not appear to match immediately. However, it should be mentioned that the various lists of disciples in other places (Matthew 10:3; Mark 3:18; Luke 6:14; Acts 1:13) do not mention Nathanael. Tradition therefore equates him with Bartholomew, *son of Ptolemy* or *son of Talmai*. In *God's Pageantry*, I have made a case for Thomas being derived from *Talmai* or from *Ptolemy*. So if Nathanael is indeed Bartholomew and if my surmise about the derivation of Thomas is correct, then the names do indeed match, though not on the surface. It seems that John is suggesting to his readers that they should dig deeper to identify 'Nathanael' and indirectly offering a hint through the name Thomas.

8. A woman named Mary is mentioned at the beginning and at the end. In both instances, there are bridal overtones to the event.

9. The emptying of the Temple by Jesus is paralleled by the emptying of the tomb.

10. Nicodemus is mentioned at the beginning and also at the end; both occasions refer to the new birth.

11. Both at the start and the finish, there is the testimony of a man named John. At the beginning John the Baptist testifies to the Bridegroom. At the end, John the apostle testifies to Jesus' last word: 'kalah', *it is finished*, or 'kallah', *my bride*.

117

9. See Brian Simmons, *John: Eternal Love* (The Passion Translation), Broadstreet Publishing Group, LLC 2014

10. John 11:2 identifies Mary, the sister of Lazarus, as the one who anointed Jesus and wiped His feet with her hair. Many scholars therefore consider that, since she is not identified as The Magdalene, then this is yet another Mary, dubbed 'Mary of Bethany'. However, I believe that she can be positively identified as Mary Magdalene— and that she acquired the name 'the Madgalene' during a name covenant with Jesus. The details of this exchange and the unusual nature of the covenant involved are covered in the previous book in this series, *Name Covenant: Invitation to Friendship*, Armour Books 2018.

11. http://www.abarim-publications.com/Meaning/ Nicodemus.html#.XFKmkywRVdg

12. For example, a preacher may say, 'It's God's desire that your entire family will be saved.' To invest intentionally in that declaration for your own family, you may throw a hundred dollars into a bucket in order to see it manifest for them. Unfortunately, the preacher's declarations frequently appeal to more carnal motives than the salvation of your family and, therefore, may draw people into the 'error of Balaam'—coming out from under covenant at a critical time. As far as I am concerned, 'trading' as currently practised is one of the most dangerous counterfeits of covenant possible. The satan, after all, was expelled from heaven for trading. (Ezekiel 28) God's covenantal love for us is insulted by the use of money in this fashion. He doesn't need our hundred dollars or even our hundred thousand dollars. He wants our entire lives.

I have read several books on trading, I have been to

several seminars and I have watched some videos. As a consequence, I have realised that the term 'trading' is often used indiscriminately, as if it sometimes means 'covenant' and sometimes not. This confusing vagueness is a minefield for anyone seeking God and tempted to choose a false refuge rather than a true one.

Covenant is essentially and radically different from trading. Covenant is about *oneness*. That's what differentiates it from contract, pledge, vow, exchange or trade. Covenant happens to be about exchanging gifts as tokens of love, so it might look like trading in some respects. But the difference is ONENESS. If I buy a car, I don't want to trade some money for a vehicle and wind up having to take care of the seller's family for life. In a trade, it's not about gifts—it's not only about exchange but, hopefully, in the final analysis, *ethical* exchange.

Much spiritual trading in my view is simply about unbelief in the atonement. It's a natural human inclination to want to help Jesus out when we've prayed and prayed and prayed and still things haven't gone the way we wanted. We are so inventive in finding ways to enhance the atonement. Repentance and forgiveness only 'work' by the grace of God. He requires them but, in truth, they don't add a single thing to the all-sufficiency of the sacrifice of Jesus. They are more about tokens of love than anything else—about telling God that, yes, broken as I am, I am committed to the relationship. And that, in my heart of hearts, I cannot believe in the atonement without wanting to 'do' something to help Jesus solve my present crisis. The only fallback position in this case is, I think, encapsulated in the petition of the Roman centurion: 'Lord, I believe—help my unbelief.'

13. See the previous volume in this series, *Name Covenant: Invitation to Friendship*, Armour Books 2018.

14. Thomas' father was a blacksmith and his surname at birth was Hemerken or 'hammerkin', *little hammer*.

15. Jackie Hill Perry quoting *Gospel Fluency* in *Gay Girl, Good God: The Story of Who I Was, and Who God Has Always Been*, B & H Books 2018

16. The different Hebrew words translated as 'atonement' often contribute to the confusion surrounding the understanding of this word. For a good analysis, see the entry in *Baker's Evangelical Dictionary of Biblical Theology*. Sometimes *atonement* is understood as a 'covering' for sin, an unfortunate term because it leads many of us to imagine a great crimson sheet hiding our sins from God. In fact, the word is closer in meaning to 'covering' in the insurance sense, although the very mention of insurance also brings up unfortunate connotations. Atonement might be conceived as having the 'cover' needed to repair the damage—the ability to 'cover' the ruinous impact on the relationship between God and man and restore it into glory. On Yom Kippur, the Day of Atonement, the emphasis was on restoring unity with God. Blood was seven times applied to the Mercy Seat—the covering for the Ark of the Covenant. The Mercy Seat—which has a name related to atonement—was in fact the meeting place of heaven and earth: where heaven and earth joined. When the blood was sprinkled heaven and earth came into union once more. The blood was a sign of reparation to overcome the separation caused by sin.

Ultimately, whatever situation the word 'atonement' is used in, it describes an object or an action which brings people back into oneness with God.

17. The eclipse occurred during the day. Therefore it cannot have been a lunar eclipse, which only happens at night. However a solar eclipse is out of the question because it was Passover—which means that the moon would have been on the opposite side of the earth to that needed to produce a solar eclipse. Besides, the total darkness of a solar eclipse lasts, at best, just a few minutes. The darkness at the time of the death of Jesus lasted for several hours.

Dealing with Python: Spirit of Constriction

Strategies for the Threshold #1

Anne Hamilton
Arpana Dev Sangamithra

On the threshold into your unique calling in life a dark spiritual sentinel waits.

Scripture names it 'Python'—it has a God-given right to be there and test your significant choices. Trying to cast it out of a situation is useless.

Paul encountered it just as the Gospel was transitioning across a major threshold: the watershed moment when Christianity moved from Asia to Europe.

This much-praised book explores the tactics of Python, as well as its agenda. It offers insight into what this spirit hopes to get from you and how you can rectify past mistakes involving this constricting, cunning enemy.

Dealing with Ziz: Spirit of Forgetting

Strategies for the Threshold #1

Anne Hamilton
Arpana Dev Sangamithra

The most significant of the threshold points of life is the doorway into God's unique calling for us. He invites us through covenant to fulfil the destiny and purpose for which we were born. However, many of us fall at the threshold, rather than pass over it. We experience unremitting constriction, wasting, retaliation and forgetting—to such a degree that it's easy to doubt the promises of God.

This pioneering work examines the spiritual implications of forgetting in relation to thresholds and covenants. Because the opposite of remembering is dismembering—dismembering of truth—the spirit of forgetting is able to bar the way into our calling.

But there is an answer.